Violin

SYLLABUS / 2013 EDITION

Message from the President

The Royal Conservatory of Music was founded in 1886 with the idea that a single institution could bind the people of a nation together with the common thread of shared musical experience. More than a century later, we continue to build and expand on this vision.

Today, The Royal Conservatory is recognized in communities across North America for outstanding service to students, teachers, and parents, as well as strict adherence to high academic standards through a variety of activities—teaching, examining, publishing, research, and community outreach.

Our students and teachers benefit from a curriculum based on more than 125 years of commitment to the highest pedagogical objectives. The strength of the curriculum is reinforced by the distinguished College of Examiners—a group of fine musicians and teachers who have been carefully selected from across Canada, the United States, and abroad for their demonstrated skill and professionalism. A rigorous examiner apprenticeship program, combined with regular evaluation procedures, ensures consistency and an examination experience of the highest quality for candidates.

As you pursue your studies or teach others, you become not only an important partner with The Royal Conservatory in the development of creativity, discipline, and goal-setting, but also an active participant, experiencing the transcendent qualities of music itself. In a society where our day-to-day lives can become rote and routine, the human need to find self-fulfillment and to engage in creative activity has never been more necessary. The Royal Conservatory will continue to be an active partner and supporter in your musical journey of self-expression and self-discovery.

Dr. Peter C. Simon
President

Contents

Getting Started

What's New?

- Preparatory examinations are now graded.
- Only one etude is required for Grade 7.
- Technical Requirements have been revised.
- The marking scheme for Technical Requirements has been revised for Grades 7 to 10.
- There is a specific memory mark deduction for Lists A, C, and D repertoire in Grades 7 to 10.
- Orchestral Excerpts now include chamber music repertoire.
- Candidates in Grade 10 have the opportunity to split the examination into two separate segments.

Visit www.examinations.rcmusic.ca to register for an examination or for further information concerning official Royal Conservatory programs.

Contact Us

- Phone: 416-408-5019 or toll-free 1-800-461-6058
- Fax: 416-408-3151

273 Bloor Street West
Toronto, ON Canada M5S 1W2

Examinations Offered

Practical Examinations

Accordion, Bassoon, Cello, Clarinet, Double Bass, Flute, French Horn, Guitar, Harp, Harpsichord, Oboe, Organ, Percussion, Piano, Recorder, Saxophone, Speech Arts and Drama, Trombone, Trumpet, Tuba, Viola, Violin, Voice

Theory Examinations

Rudiments, Harmony, Keyboard Harmony, History, Counterpoint, Analysis

Musicianship Examinations

Junior, Intermediate, Senior

About Us

The Royal Conservatory

The Royal Conservatory is one of the largest and most respected music education institutions in the world. Providing the definitive standard of excellence in music education through its curricula, examinations, performances, and teacher education programs, The Royal Conservatory has had a substantial impact on the lives of millions of people globally.

Notable alumni include:
- Randy Bachman
- Isabel Bayrakdarian
- Russell Braun
- Martin Beaver
- Measha Brueggergosman
- Adrienne Clarkson
- Bruce Cockburn
- Naida Cole
- David Foster
- Glenn Gould
- Angela Hewitt
- Norman Jewison
- Diana Krall
- Gordon Lightfoot
- Lois Marshall
- Sarah McLachlan
- Jon Kimura Parker
- Oscar Peterson
- Adrianne Pieczonka
- Paul Shaffer
- St. Lawrence String Quartet
- Teresa Stratas
- Shania Twain
- Jon Vickers

Visit rcmusic.ca to learn more about the history of The Royal Conservatory.

The Royal Conservatory Examinations

The Royal Conservatory provides a recognized standard of musical success through an effectively sequenced course of study and individual student examinations, from preparatory to advanced grades. Over 100,000 examinations are conducted annually in 260 communities across Canada.

The College of Examiners

Examiners are highly trained professional musicians and theorists from across North America. All examiners complete an Examiner Apprenticeship Program before being admitted to the College of Examiners. Professional development and training continues throughout each examiner's career to ensure consistent examination standards across North America.

Read about the College of Examiners, including examiner biographies, at www.examinations.rcmusic.ca

The Frederick Harris Music Co., Limited

As The Royal Conservatory's publishing division, The Frederick Harris Music Co., Limited produces The Royal Conservatory's renowned Syllabi and related teaching and examining materials for individual instruments, voice, and theoretical subjects.

Additional programs of The Royal Conservatory are delivered through the following divisions:
- **The Glenn Gould School** provides professional training in music for gifted young artists at the undergraduate and graduate levels.
- **The Young Artists Performance Academy** provides supportive, comprehensive training for promising young musicians aged nine to eighteen.
- **The Royal Conservatory School** provides acclaimed early childhood music education programs, music classes, and private lessons for people of all ages and stages of musical literacy.
- **Learning Through the Arts®** supports excellence in public education programs by using the arts to enhance learning.
- The **Performing Arts Division** programs superb performances and events in The Royal Conservatory's three venues: Koerner Hall, Mazzoleni Concert Hall in historic Ihnatowycz Hall, and the Conservatory Theatre.
- **The Royal Conservatory Music Development Program** promotes and expands musical activity in the United States and makes the study of music a central part of the lives of all Americans.

Examination Requirements

Certificate Program Overview

A progressive assessment program for every examination candidate

Internationally recognized certificates are awarded for successful completion of each practical grade and the required co-requisite theory examination(s). Internationally recognized diplomas are awarded for successful completion of the ARCT practical examination and the required co-requisite examinations in theory and piano. Candidates may enter the Certificate Program at any practical grade from Preparatory to Grade 10. The following table summarizes the examinations required for each certificate.

Certificates	Examinations Required
Preparatory Violin	Preparatory Violin
Grade 1 Violin	Grade 1 Violin
Grade 2 Violin	Grade 2 Violin
Grade 3 Violin	Grade 3 Violin
Grade 4 Violin	Grade 4 Violin
Grade 5 Violin	Grade 5 Violin; Basic Rudiments
Grade 6 Violin	Grade 6 Violin; Intermediate Rudiments
Grade 7 Violin	Grade 7 Violin; Advanced Rudiments
Grade 8 Violin	Grade 8 Violin; Advanced Rudiments
Grade 9 Violin	Grade 9 Violin; Advanced Rudiments; Basic Harmony/Basic Keyboard Harmony; History 1: An Overview
Grade 10 Violin	Grade 10 Violin; Advanced Rudiments; Intermediate Harmony/Intermediate Keyboard Harmony; History 1: An Overview; History 2: Middle Ages to Classical

Diploma	Examinations Required
ARCT in Violin Performance	ARCT in Violin Performance; History 3: 19th Century to Present; any *two* of: Advanced Harmony/Advanced Keyboard Harmony, *or* Analysis, *or* Counterpoint; Grade 6 Piano
Teacher's ARCT	Teacher's ARCT (Parts 1, 2, and 3); History 3: 19th Century to Present; any *two* of: Advanced Harmony/Advanced Keyboard Harmony, *or* Analysis, *or* Counterpoint; Grade 8 Piano *For current information concerning Teacher's ARCT requirements, please visit www.rcmusic.ca.*

Theory Examinations

Essential Tools for Musical Development

- Violin candidates are encouraged to begin theory and piano studies as early as possible.
- Beginning at Grade 5, candidates must complete the required theory examinations in order to receive Practical Examination Certificates.

See the current edition of the *Theory Syllabus* for detailed theory examination requirements.

Overview of Theoretical Subjects

The following table lists all of the written theory examinations in the Certificate Program with brief details, including the length of the examination and a summary description of the content.

Subject	Theory Examination Title
Rudiments	Preparatory Rudiments (1 hour) – Building blocks of music notation
	Basic Rudiments (1 hour) – Elements of music for the beginner
	Intermediate Rudiments (2 hours) – Continuation of basic rudiments
	Advanced Rudiments (2 hours) – Continuation of intermediate rudiments and preparation for harmony
Harmony and Counterpoint	Introductory Harmony (2 hours) – Chord symbols; non-chord tones; elementary four-part and melodic writing
	Basic Harmony (3 hours) – Four-part writing; melodic composition; harmonic and structural analysis in major and minor keys *or* Basic Keyboard Harmony (20 minutes) – Melodic improvisation; keyboard-style harmonization; accompaniment; melodic transposition; harmonic and structural analysis
	Intermediate Harmony (3 hours) – Four-part writing and melodic composition in major and minor keys; modulation; harmonic and structural analysis of musical forms *or* Intermediate Keyboard Harmony (25 minutes) – Melodic improvisation; keyboard-style harmonization; modulation; accompaniment; melodic transposition; harmonic analysis; C-clef reading
	Counterpoint (3 hours) – Composition and analysis of simple counterpoint in Baroque style
	Advanced Harmony (3 hours) – Advanced harmonic and contrapuntal techniques *or* Advanced Keyboard Harmony (30 minutes) – Melodic improvisation; keyboard-style harmonization; figured bass; accompaniment; melodic and orchestral transposition; score reading
Analysis	Analysis (3 hours) – Advanced harmonic and structural analysis of musical forms
History	History 1: An Overview (3 hours) – Introduction to styles, composers, and music from 1600 to the present
	History 2: Middle Ages to Classical (3 hours) – Styles, composers, and music of the Medieval, Renaissance, Baroque, Rococo, and Classical periods
	History 3: 19th Century to Present (3 hours) – Styles, composers, and music of the Romantic era to the present

Preparing for a Theory Examination

- Theory examinations test music theory and knowledge of music history in a formal classroom setting, generally with a written examination.
- *Official Examination Papers*, available at music retailers, are published annually by The Frederick Harris Music Co., Limited to aid with examination preparation.

Co-requisites and Prerequisites

The following table summarizes all the co-requisite and prerequisite examinations required to obtain certificates for Grades 5 to 10 and diplomas for the ARCT in Violin Performance or the Teacher's ARCT. There are no prerequisite or co-requisite theory examinations for Preparatory to Grade 4. However, it is recommended that students complete Preparatory Rudiments prior to Basic Rudiments. Similarly, it is recommended that students complete Introductory Harmony prior to Basic Harmony.

Candidates for the ARCT in Violin Performance or the Teacher's ARCT will be required to complete the following theory examinations: History 3: 19th Century to Present, and *two* of the following three examinations: Advanced Harmony/Advanced Keyboard Harmony, *or* Counterpoint, *or* Analysis. The selection of these examinations and the order in which they are taken is at the discretion of the candidate.

Candidates for the ARCT in Violin Performance must complete co-requisite theory examinations and the Grade 6 Piano examination before or within five years of the original practical examination to be eligible for the Diploma.

Candidates must complete prerequisite examinations at least one session prior to attempting the ARCT in Violin Performance. For up-to-date information on the Teacher's ARCT please consult www.rcmusic.ca.

Grade	5	6	7	8	9	10	ARCT in Performance	Teacher's ARCT
Required Examinations (C = Co-requisite P = Prerequisite)								
Basic Rudiments	C							
Intermediate Rudiments		C						
Advanced Rudiments			C	C	C	C	P	P
Basic Harmony					C			
Intermediate Harmony						C	P	P
Any *two* of: Advanced Harmony, *or* Counterpoint, *or* Analysis							C	C
History 1: An Overview					C	C	P	P
History 2: Middle Ages to Classical						C	P	P
History 3: 19th Century to Present							C	C
Grade 10 Practical							P	P
Grade 6 Piano							C	
Grade 8 Piano								C
Alternative Examinations								
Basic Keyboard Harmony (can be substituted for Basic Harmony)					C			
Intermediate Keyboard Harmony (can be substituted for Intermediate Harmony)						C	P	P
Advanced Keyboard Harmony (can be substituted for Advanced Harmony)							C	C
Junior Musicianship (can be substituted for Grade 8 Ear Tests)				C				
Intermediate Musicianship (can be substituted for Grade 9 Ear Tests)					C			
Senior Musicianship (can be substituted for Grade 10 and Teacher's ARCT Ear Tests)						C		C

Examination Repertoire

The *Violin Syllabus, 2013 Edition* lists the repertoire for violin examinations. Information given for each item includes:

- the composer
- the title of the selection
- the larger work of which the selection is a part (where applicable)
- an anthology or collection in which the selection can be found (where applicable)
- performance directions (where applicable) indicating the section(s) of a work to be prepared
- the publisher of a suggested edition (where applicable)

Names of publishers are indicated by an assigned abbreviation. Please see p. 86 for a list of publishers with their abbreviations.

Syllabus Repertoire Lists

At each grade, candidates are encouraged to choose a balanced and varied examination program that includes a variety of musical styles and keys. The repertoire for each grade is divided into lists, according to genre or stylistic period.

Preparatory, Grade 1, and Grade 2

List A: Pieces in a Slower Tempo
List B: Pieces in a Faster Tempo

Grade 3

List A: Repertoire in Baroque and Classical Styles
List B: Traditional and Romantic Repertoire
List C: Repertoire Composed After 1930

Grade 4

List A: Concertos, Sonatinas, and Fantasias
List B: Repertoire in Baroque Style
List C: Concert Repertoire

Grade 5, Grade 6, and Grade 7

List A: Concertos, *Airs variés,* and Fantasias
List B: Sonatas and Sonatinas
List C: Concert Repertoire

Grade 8

List A: Concertos, *Airs variés,* and Fantasias
List B: Sonatas and Sonatinas
List C: Concert Repertoire
List D: Unaccompanied Repertoire

Grade 9

List A: Concertos and *Airs variés*
List B: Sonatas and Sonatinas
List C: Concert Repertoire
List D: Unaccompanied Repertoire of Johann Sebastian Bach

Grade 10

List A: Concertos
List B: Sonatas
List C: Concert Repertoire
List D: Unaccompanied Repertoire of Johann Sebastian Bach

ARCT in Violin Performance

List A: Concertos
List B: Sonatas
List C: Concert Repertoire
List D: Unaccompanied Repertoire

Da Capo Signs and Repeats

- When performing repertoire in an examination, candidates should observe *da capo* and *dal segno* signs, unless stated otherwise in the *Violin Syllabus, 2013 Edition*.
- Repeat signs should be observed *only* if indicated in the *Violin Syllabus, 2013 Edition* or in *Violin Series, 2013 Edition*.

Memory

At Preparatory through Grade 6, six marks are awarded for the memorization of repertoire.

- Three marks are awarded for each repertoire selection performed by memory in Preparatory and Grades 1 and 2.
- Two marks are awarded for each repertoire selection performed by memory in Grades 3 and 4.
- In Grades 5 and 6, three marks are awarded for each repertoire selection from Lists A and C performed by memory. List B selections need not be performed by memory, and no extra marks will be awarded for memorization.

At Grade 7 through ARCT, candidates are expected to perform all repertoire by memory, with the exception of List B selections, which do not need to be memorized.

- A memory mark deduction of 10% per repertoire selection will be made for pieces from Lists A, C, and D that are performed with music.
- List B selections need not be performed by memory, and no extra marks will be awarded for memorization.

Candidates must provide their own collaborative pianist in order for the examination to proceed.

Accompaniment

All selections requiring accompaniment must be performed with piano accompaniment only. No other instruments are permitted. Recorded accompaniment is not permitted.

Candidates must provide their own collaborative pianist. Collaborative pianists are permitted in the examination room only while they are playing accompaniments for the candidate.

Repertoire Substitutions

Violin candidates at Grades 1 through ARCT have the option of substituting *one* repertoire selection at each examination with a selection of their own choice. Repertoire substitutions for Violin fall under the following categories.

Syllabus Substitutions

Candidates in Grade 1 through 10 may substitute *one* repertoire selection from the grade immediately above without prior approval. The repertoire substitution must normally be chosen from the corresponding List of the grade immediately above the candidate's official grade. For example, a Grade 5 List A selection may be performed in place of a Grade 4 List A selection.

Please note that the performance of repertoire substitutions chosen from a higher grade will be evaluated at the standard of the higher grade. **NOTE: No *Syllabus* substitution is allowed for Grade 10 List D repertoire.**

Non-Syllabus Substitutions Requiring Approval

Violin candidates may apply to substitute one repertoire selection not listed in the *Violin Syllabus, 2013 Edition* with a work that is comparable in style and difficulty. The substitute repertoire selection must be of comparable length and musical quality to selections in the specified List. Approval of such selections is based on the suitability of the style and the level of difficulty of the substitute composition.

Candidates wishing to include a substitute selection on their examination programs must complete an Examination Substitute Piece Request Form (available at www.examinations.rcmusic.ca) by the examination registration deadline. Candidates are advised to prepare an alternate work in case the request is denied.

- Send the completed form together with the appropriate fee and a copy of the substitute piece to The Royal Conservatory Examinations. (Photocopies used for this purpose should be marked "For Approval Only"; these copies will be destroyed once a decision has been made.) Any published music submitted will be returned to the candidate along with the approval form.
- Bring the approved Examination Substitute Piece Request Form to your examination and give it to the examiner.
- Please note that marks will be deducted from the final examination mark for any unapproved Non-*Syllabus* substitution or for any *Syllabus* substitution that does not follow the guidelines provided above.

NOTE: In Grades 8, 9, 10, and ARCT, *Non-Syllabus* substitutions are not permitted for List D selections.

Orchestral Excerpts

All orchestral excerpts listed in the *Violin Syllabus, 2013 Edition* are included in *Violin Series, 2013 Edition: Orchestral Excerpts*. Alternatively, candidates may select the specified passages from standard violin orchestral parts.

Candidates are expected to play chords as they would in an orchestral setting. Unless specifically marked "non divisi," candidates should play the upper note only, or the upper two notes of three- or four-note chords.

Orchestral excerpts need not be memorized, and no extra marks will be awarded for memorization. For further details on examination requirements for orchestral excerpts, please consult the listings for each grade.

Technical Requirements

Etudes

A selection of etudes for Preparatory though Grade 8 is published in *Violin Series, 2013 Edition: Violin Technique and Etudes* (Preparatory–4 and 5–8). Etudes need not be memorized and no extra marks will be awarded for memorization. For further details on examination requirements for etudes, please consult the listings for each grade.

Technical Tests

Complete technical tests for levels Preparatory through Grade 8 are published in *Violin Series, 2013 Edition: Violin Technique and Etudes* (Preparatory–4 and 5–8). Technical tests (scales, arpeggios, and double stops) must be played from memory. No marks will be awarded for technical tests that are not performed from memory. For further details on examination requirements for technical tests, please consult the listings for each grade.

General Instructions

- The examiner will choose a representative sampling of items on the technical requirements list.
- Metronome speeds are intended as a guideline. The tempo should be compatible with the required number of notes per bow, a clear and sonorous tone, controlled rhythm, and precise intonation.
- Vibrato is not recommended. If used, it should be limited to final tonic notes.
- The fingering shown in *Violin Series, 2013 Edition: Violin Technique and Etudes* is recommended but not compulsory. Any logical fingering pattern is acceptable.
- One- and two-octave scales must be played with the patterns shown in the *Violin Syllabus, 2013 Edition*.
- Three-octave scales from Grades 5 through 8 may be played with either of the following patterns, provided they are played with the required number of notes per bow as stipulated in the *Violin Syllabus, 2013 Edition*. Candidates in Grades 9 and 10 may use either of the following patterns, or the Carl Flesch patterns.

Pattern A–Galamian Pattern

Pattern B

Grade-by-Grade Requirements

Preparatory

Candidates at the Preparatory level are expected to exhibit developing bow control and some understanding of bow division. There should be evidence of a steady, rhythmic pulse. Whole steps and half steps should be well defined. Good posture and hand set-up are important factors.

Preparatory Requirements	Marks
Repertoire	**60**
one selection from List A	27
one selection from List B	27
Memory (3 marks per repertoire selection)	6
Technical Requirements	**30**
Etudes: *one* etude from the *Syllabus* list	15
Technical Tests	15
– scales	
– arpeggios	
Ear Tests	**10**
Clapback	5
Playback	5
Total possible marks (pass = 60)	**100**
Theory Co-requisite	
None	

Repertoire

Please see "Examination Repertoire" on p. 9 for important information regarding this section of the examination.

Candidates must prepare *two* contrasting selections by two different composers: *one* from List A and *one* from List B.

Bullets used to denote selections for examination purposes:
- ● one selection
- ▶ selection is found in *Violin Series, 2013 Edition: Preparatory Violin Repertoire* FHM

List A

Pieces in a Slower Tempo

Traditional
- ● Go Tell Aunt Rhody (in *Suzuki Violin School, Revised Edition,* 1 ALF)

Archer, Violet
Three Little Studies for Violin and Piano CMC
- ● Waltz (no. 3)

Twelve Miniatures WAT; CMC
- ▶ On Tiptoe

Bayly, Thomas H.
- ● Long, Long Ago (in *Suzuki Violin School, Revised Edition,* 1 ALF)

Bennett, Richard Rodney
Up Bow, Down Bow NOV
- ● Serenade

Birston, Harold
Excursions for Violin FHM
- ▶ In Ancient Times

Blachford, Frank
- ▶ Berceuse FHM

Colledge, Katherine, and Hugh Colledge
Waggon Wheels B&H
- ● Goldfish Bowl
- ▶ Nightingale
- ● Waterfall

Coulthard, Jean
- ▶ The Climb Up Mount Royal (in *A La Jeunesse* CMC)

de Keyser, Paul
Violin Playtime, 1 FAB
- ● The Bells of St. Basil's
- ▶ Poème

Hayes, Philip
- ▶ Canon (arr. Paul de Keyser in *The Young Violinist's Repertoire,* 1 FAB)

Huws Jones, Edward
The Really Easy Violin Book FAB
- ● Dinosaur Plod

Norton, Christopher
Microjazz Violin Collection, 1 B&H)
- ● Up the Scale

Rose, Michael
- ▶ Song

Telfer, Nancy
Leading a Dog's Life CMC
- ● Time for a Nap

List B
Pieces in a Faster Tempo

Traditional
- ● May Song (in *Suzuki Violin School, Revised Edition,* 1 ALF)
- ● O Come, Little Children (in *Suzuki Violin School, Revised Edition,* 1 ALF)
- ▶ The Old Woman and The Peddler (arr. Akiko Kinney FHM)
- ▶ Playing Ball (arr. Stephen Chatman FHM)
- ● Song of the Wind (in *Suzuki Violin School, Revised Edition,* 1 ALF)

Barratt, Carol
Bravo! Violin B&H
- ● Round Dance
- ▶ Quirk

Birston, Harold
Excursions for Violin FHM
- ● I'm Crazybusy, I'm Tired
- ▶ The Old Jalopy
  - → with repeat

Colledge, Katherine, and Hugh Colledge
Waggon Wheels B&H
- ● Bell-ringers
- ▶ Knickerbocker Glory
- ● Polka Dots

Coulthard, Jean
- ● Let's Play (in *The Encore Series for Violin & Piano,* 2 FHM)

Ethridge, Jean
- ▶ The Subway Train FHM

Huws Jones, Edward
The Really Easy Violin Book FAB
- ● Spine Chiller
- ▶ Tap Dance

Janáček, Leoš, arr.
- ▶ Konopě (The Old City) (transc. Leoš Faltus in *Mährische Tänze für Violine und Klavier* UNI)

Kabalevsky, Dmitri
- ▶ Peter (transc. Konstantin Fortunatov in *Kabalevsky: Albumstücke* PET)

Krasev, A.
- ▶ Pony Trot (in *The Young Violinist's Repertoire,* 1 FAB)

Nelson, Sheila M.
Piece by Piece, 1 B&H
- ▶ Flag Dance
- ● Over the Moon

Rose, Michael
- ▶ March

Suzuki, Shin'ichi
- ● Allegro (in *Suzuki Violin School, Revised Edition,* 1 ALF)

Technical Requirements

Please see "Technical Requirements" on p. 11 for important information regarding this section of the examination.

Etudes

Candidates must prepare *one* etude from the following list.

Bullets used to denote selections for examination purposes:
- ● one selection
- ▶ selection is found in *Violin Series, 2013 Edition: Violin Technique and Etudes Preparatory–4* FHM

Anderson, Gerald E. and Robert S. Frost
All for Strings: A Comprehensive String Method, 1 KJO
- ▶ D Scale Waltz

Avsharian, Evelyn
Fun with Basics: Children's Music Series CHD
- ● *one* of nos. 1, 3, 7

Cohen, Mary
Superstudies for Violin 1 FAB
- ▶ Blast Off! (no. 1)
- ● Robots Rocking at the Microchip Ball (no. 5)

de Keyser, Paul
Violin Playtime Studies FAB
- ● Birdsong (no. 5)
- ● The Bouncing Ball (no. 12)
- ● Galloping Arpeggios (no. 11)
- ● G String Ländler (no. 9)
- ● The Little Jester (no. 13)
- ● Tick Tock Quavers (no. 7)

Donkin, Christine
Get Fiddlin'! FHM
- ● Beaver Mines (no. 1)

Givens, Shirley
Adventures in Violinland, 1F GIV
- ▶ Aren't You Glad?
- ▶ Marching Notes

Adventures in Violinland, 2B GIV
- ● The Laughing Fit
- ● Lovely Melody
- ● The Mountain Train
- ● On My Toes
- ● The Riveter
- ● Two of Us

Harris, Paul
Improve Your Scales!, 1–2 FAB
- ● Acrobatic Armadillos
- ● Delicate Dance
- ▶ Dragon Drama!

RT, Zav, arr.
Fiddleworks, 1 FHM
- ▶ Cripple Creek

Technical Tests

Please see "Technical Tests" on p. 11 for important information regarding this section of the examination. Candidates must play scales and arpeggios from memory.

Scales	Keys	Range	Tempo	Bowing
Major	D, A	1 octave start on open string	♩ = 60	♩♩
Arpeggios				
Major	D, A	1 octave start on open string	♩ = 60	♩♩♩

Ear Tests

Clapback

Candidates will choose to either clap or tap the rhythm of a short melody after the examiner has played it *twice* on the piano.

Time Signatures	Approximate Length
2/4 3/4	two to four measures

Example only

Playback

Candidates will be asked to play back a melody on the violin, based on the first three notes of a major scale. The examiner will name the key, play the tonic triad *once*, and play the melody *twice* on the piano.

Beginning Note	Keys	Approximate Length
tonic	D, A major	four notes

Example only

Grade 1

Candidates in Grade 1 should be able to play whole bows, slurs, *legato*, and *staccato* strokes. There should be evidence of a steady, rhythmic pulse. Tone should be clear and some variety in dynamic levels should be present. Tonality should be well centered.

Grade 1 Requirements	Marks
Repertoire *one* selection from List A *one* selection from List B **Memory** (3 marks per repertoire selection)	**60** 27 27 6
Technical Requirements Etudes: *two* etudes from the *Syllabus* list Technical Tests – scales – arpeggios – double stops	**30** 15 15
Ear Tests Clapback Playback	**10** 5 5
Total possible marks (pass = 60)	**100**
Theory Co-requisite None	

Repertoire

Please see "Examination Repertoire" on p. 9 for important information regarding this section of the examination.

Candidates must prepare *two* contrasting selections by two different composers, *one* from List A and *one* from List B.

Bullets used to denote selections for examination purposes:

- ● one selection
- ▶ selection is found in *Violin Series, 2013 Edition: Violin Repertoire 1* FHM

List A
Pieces in a Slower Tempo

Traditional
- ● All Through the Night (arr. Barbara Barber in *Solos for Young Violinists,* 1 ALF)
- ▶ Un Canadien errant (*The Wandering Canadian*) (arr. David Duke in *The Encore Series for Violin & Piano,* 2 FHM)
- ● On the Wing (arr. Carol Barratt in *Bravo! Violin* B&H)

Bartók Béla
- ● Andante (arr. Ede Zathureczky, no. 8 in *For Children (Gyermekeknek)* EMB)

Birston, Harold
Excursions for Violin FHM
- ▶ March of the Elephants

Carse, Adam
Fiddle Fancies S&B
- ● Bluebell Chimes
- ▶ Sweet Sorrow

Cofalik, Antoni, and Romuald Twardowski
At the Zoo BAR
- ● The Bear (Der Bär)

Colledge, Katherine, and Hugh Colledge
Waggon Wheels B&H
- ● Bow Ties!
- ● Full Moon

Coulthard, Jean
- ▶ Grandfather Tells a Witch Story
- ▶ A Song for Bedtime (in *A La Jeunesse* CMC)

Cui, César
- ▶ From My Homeland (arr. Paul de Keyser and Fanny Waterman in *The Young Violinist's Repertoire,* 3 FAB)

Donkin, Christine
Costume Party FHM
- ● The Sasquatch
- ▶ The Tooth Fairy

Elgar, Edward
Six Very Easy Pieces in the First Position, op. 22 FAB; BOS
- ▶ Andante in C Major (no. 1)

Handel, George Frideric
- ▶ Air from *Rinaldo* (arr. Kathleen Wood FHM)
- ● Chorus from *Judas Maccabaeus* (in *Suzuki Violin School, Revised Edition,* 2 ALF)

Huws Jones, Edward
The Really Easy Violin Book FAB
- ● Skye

Kabalevsky, Dmitri
Twenty Pieces for Violin and Piano, op. 80 SCH; SIK
- ▶ A Song (no. 6)

Lawes, Henry
- ● A Canzonet (arr. Thomas Dunhill in *Fiddler's Choice,* 1 ABR)

Popp, Paulette, arr. Christine Gale
- ▶ The Plucky Snake

Sugár, Rezso
Song and Dance (in *Violin Music for Beginners,* 1 EMB)
- ● complete

Suzuki, Shin'ichi
- ● Andantino (in *Suzuki Violin School, Revised Edition,* 1 ALF)

Telfer, Nancy
If Flowers Could Speak CMC
- ● The Lonely Sunflower

List B
Pieces in a Faster Tempo

Anonymous
- ▶ Caterpillar! Caterpillar! (arr. Akiko Kinney FHM)
- ● Contredanse (in *Violin Playtime,* 2 FAB)
- ● Minuet (attr. William Duncombe, arr. Carol Barratt, in *Bravo! Violin* B&H)
- ● Untitled Reel 1 (arr. John Beckwith, in *Eight Miniatures from the Allen Ash Manuscript* FHM)

Archer, Violet
Twelve Miniatures WAT; CMC
- ● Jig

Bach, Johann Sebastian
- ● Minuet 1 from Suite in G Minor, BWV 822 (arr. in *Suzuki Violin School, Revised Edition,* 1 ALF)

Bartók Béla
- ● Allegro non troppo (arr. Ede Zathureczky, no. 1 in *For Children (Gyermekeknek)* EMB)
- ▶ Dance (Táncdal) (arr. Ede Zathureczky, no. 5 in *For Children (Gyermekeknek)* EMB)

Carse, Adam
The Fiddler's Nursery S&B
- ● A Bumpkin's Dance
- ● At Dawn
- ● Dance Steps
- ● Minuet

Cofalik, Antoni, and Romuald Twardowski
At the Zoo BAR
- ● The Kangaroo (Das Känguru)
- ● Two Little Donkeys (Zwei kleine Esel)

Colledge, Katherine, and Hugh Colledge
Fast Forward B&H
- ● Hallowe'en
- ● Singapore Sunset

Waggon Wheels B&H
- ▶ Lollipop Man

Donkin, Christine
Costume Party FHM
- ▶ The Cowboy
- ● The Magician
- ● The Pirate

Elgar, Edward
Six Very Easy Pieces in the First Position, op. 22 FAB; BOS
- ● Allegretto in C Major (no. 2)

Fleming, Robert
- ● Scotty Lad CMC

Huws Jones, Edward
The Really Easy Violin Book FAB
- ● Boogie
- ▶ Pipe and Tabor

Janáček, Leoš, arr.
- ▶ Moravian Dance (Dymák) (transc. Leoš Faltus in *Mährische Tänze für Violine und Klavier* UNI)

Kabalevsky, Dmitri
Twenty Pieces for Violin and Piano, op. 80 SCH; SIK
- ● Dance Song (no. 10)
- ● Games (no. 3)
- ▶ March (no. 5)

Lumsden, Caroline, and Ben Attwood
Wizard's Potion PET
- ▶ Dizzy Lizzy Lightweight
- ● Jump Slimy Toad

Mackay, Neil
Four Modern Dance Tunes S&B
- ▶ Cha-Cha
  → omit repeat

Matz, Rudolph
A Spring Day – Seven Short Pieces
- ● With Friends UMP

Murray, Eleanor, and Phyllis Tate
Tunes for My Violin B&H
- ● The Gypsy Fiddler

Nelson, Sheila M.
Piece by Piece, 1 B&H
- ▶ Whirlpool Waltz

Piece by Piece, 2 B&H
- ● Dance of the Minor Thirds
- ● Merry Go Round

Norton, Christopher
Microjazz Violin Collection, 1 B&H
- ▶ Snooker Table

Schumann, Robert
- ● The Happy Farmer (arr. in *Suzuki Violin School, Revised Edition,* 1 ALF)
- ▶ Soldier's March, op. 68, no. 2 (arr. FHM)
  → with repeat

Suzuki, Shin'ichi
- ● Allegretto (in *Suzuki Violin School, Revised Edition,* 1 ALF)

Technical Requirements

Please see "Technical Requirements" on p. 11 for important information regarding this section of the examination.

Etudes

Candidates must prepare *two* technically contrasting etudes from the following list.

Bullets used to denote selections for examination purposes:

- ● one selection
- ▶ selection is found in *Violin Series, 2013 Edition: Violin Technique and Etudes Preparatory—4* FHM

Anonymous
- ▶ Bow Division FHM

Cohen, Mary
Superstudies for Violin, 1 FAB
- ● Rocking Rowboats (no. 6)
- ● Space Walk (no. 4)

Superstudies for Violin, 2 FAB
- ▶ Gliding Along at the Octopus Ball (no. 9)

de Keyser, Paul
Violin Playtime Studies FAB
- ● Chugging Along (no. 25)
- ● Courageous Crotchets (no. 10)
- ● Legato Leaps (no. 14)
- ● Puppet on Two Strings (no. 8)
- ● The See-Saw (no. 2)

Donkin, Christine
Get Fiddlin'! FHM
- ● Athabasca (no. 5)
- ● Crowsnest Pass (no. 2)
- ▶ Nojack (no. 14)

Entezami, Ramin
Melodious Etudes in First Position FIS
- ▶ The Little Eel (no. 9)

Gale, Christine
- ▶ The Sulky Sailor

Givens, Shirley
Adventures in Violinland, 2B GIV
- ▶ Tuning Up!

Harris, Paul
Improve Your Scales!, 1–2 FAB
- ● Amusement Arcade
- ● Apish Antics
- ● Gentle Genie

Kinsey, Herbert
Elementary Progressive Studies, set 1 ABR
- ● *one* of nos. 1, 2, 7

Metz, Louis
Vioolmethode, 2 B&V
- ● no. 48

Romberg, Bernhard Heinrich
- ▶ Andante (arr. A. Baird Knechtel)

Suzuki, Shin'ichi
Suzuki Violin School, Revised Edition, 1 ALF
- ● Etude (with sixteenth-note variation)
- ● Perpetual Motion in A Major (with sixteenth-note variation)
- ● Perpetual Motion in D Major (with sixteenth-note variation)

Telfer, Nancy
Ready to Go? CMC
- ▶ Little Red Sportscar

Technical Tests

Please see "Technical Tests" on p. 11 for important information regarding this section of the examination.

Candidates must play all scales, arpeggios, and double stops from memory. Refer to *Violin Series, 2013 Edition: Violin Technique and Etudes Preparatory–4* FHM for required patterns.

Scales	Keys	Range	Tempo	Bowing
Major	G	2 octaves	♩ = 69	♩♩
	C	1 octave		
Harmonic Minor	A, D	1 octave start on open string		
Arpeggios				
Major	G	2 octaves	♩ = 69	♩♩♩
Major	C	1 octave		
Minor	A, D	1 octave start on open string		
Double Stops*				
Exercise on Open Strings			♩ = 69	𝅗𝅥

*See *Violin Series, 2013 Edition: Violin Technique and Etudes Preparatory–4* FHM.

Ear Tests

Clapback

Candidates will choose to either clap or tap the rhythm of a short melody after the examiner has played it *twice* on the piano.

Time Signatures	Approximate Length
$\frac{2}{4}$ $\frac{3}{4}$	three to four measures

Example only

1

2

Playback

Candidates will be asked to play back a melody on the violin, based on the first three notes of a major scale. The melody may contain repeated notes and a leap of a 3rd. The examiner will name the key, play the tonic triad *once*, and play the melody *twice* on the piano.

Beginning Note	Keys	Approximate Length
tonic	D, A major	four notes

Example only

1

2

Grade 2

Candidates in Grade 2 should be able to play in all parts of the bow with good control and should be able to execute slurs, *legato*, and *staccato* strokes. Tone should be clear and some variety in dynamic levels should be present. Whole steps and half steps should be clearly defined in 1st and 3rd positions and tonality should be well centred in both major and minor keys.

Grade 2 Requirements	Marks
Repertoire	**60**
one selection from List A	27
one selection from List B	27
Memory (3 marks per repertoire selection)	6
Technical Requirements	**30**
Etudes: *two* etudes from the *Syllabus* list	15
Technical Tests	15
– scales	
– arpeggios	
– double stops	
Ear Tests	**10**
Clapback	3
Intervals	3
Playback	4
Total possible marks (pass = 60)	**100**
Theory Co-requisite	
None	

Repertoire

Please see “Examination Repertoire” on p. 9 for important information regarding this section of the examination.

Candidates must prepare *two* contrasting selections by two different composers, *one* from List A and *one* from List B.

Bullets used to denote selections for examination purposes:

- ● one selection
- ▶ selection is found in *Violin Series, 2013 Edition: Violin Repertoire 2* FHM

List A
Pieces in a Slower Tempo

Archer, Violet
Twelve Miniatures WAT; CMC
- ● In Church

Bach, Johann Sebastian
- ● Musette from English Suite No. 3, BWV 808 (arr. in *Suzuki Violin School, Revised Edition,* 2 ALF)

Barnes, Milton
Three Folk Dances CMC
- ▶ Folk Dance No. 2

Bartók, Béla
- ● Chanson du Vagabond (Betyár Nóta) (arr. Ede Zathureczky, no. 4 in *For Children (Gyermekeknek)* EMB)

Bayly, Thomas H.
- ● Long, Long Ago (with variation) (in *Suzuki Violin School, Revised Edition,* 2 ALF)

Beethoven, Ludwig van
- ● Abschied (arr. Alfred Moffat in *Old Fiddle Pieces,* OTT)

Bennett, Richard Rodney
Up Bow, Down Bow NOV
- ● A Little Elegy
- ▶ A Quiet Conversation

Colledge, Katherine, and Hugh Colledge
Fast Forward B&H
- ● Snake Charmer
- ▶ Wondering

Shooting Stars B&H
- ▶ The Misty Isle

Coulthard, Jean
- ● A Little Sorrow (in *The Encore Series for Violin & Piano,* 2 FHM)

Donkin, Christine
Costume Party FHM
- ● The Acrobat

Elgar, Edward
Six Very Easy Pieces in the First Position, op. 22 FAB; BOS
- ● Andante in A Minor (no. 3)
- ▶ Andantino in G Major (no. 4)

Ethridge, Jean
- ▶ Cradle Song (in *The Encore Series for Violin & Piano,* 2 FHM)

Halvorsen, Johan
- ▶ Mélodie (arr. Warren Mould FHM)

Heins, Donald
The Bell Boy Suite FHM
- ▶ Prelude: “Calling Mr. Eccles”
- ▶ Aria *and* Bourrée

Hook, James
- ● Tempo di menuetto (arr. Alfred Moffat in *Old Masters for Young Players,* 3 OTT)

Kabalevsky, Dmitri
Twenty Pieces for Violin and Piano, op. 80 SCH; SIK
- ▶ Dreamers (no. 19)
- ● Melody (no. 14)

Laoureux, Nicolas
- ● Petite Berceuse FRB

McDougall, Barbara
- ▶ Tall Ships (arr. Judith McIvor FHM)

Murray, Eleanor, and Phyllis Tate
Tunes for My Violin B&H
- ● Song of the Roads
- ● The Swan

Pracht, Robert
Twelve Easy Pieces, op. 12 BMC
- ● Romance

Rameau, Jean-Philippe
- ● Two Sarabandes from *Premier livre de pièces de clavecin* (arr. Alfred Moffat in *Old Fiddle Pieces* OTT)

Tchaikovsky, Pyotr Il'yich
- ▶ Mélodie antique française (Old French Song) from *Album pour enfants* (arr. FHM)

Telfer, Nancy
If Flowers Could Speak CMC
- ● Dance of the Peonies

List B
Pieces in a Faster Tempo

Traditional
- ● Maytime (arr. Paul de Keyser and Fanny Waterman, in *The Young Violinist's Repertoire*, 3 FAB)

Archer, Violet
Twelve Miniatures WAT; CMC
- ● Waltzing

Babell, William
- ● Two Matelottes (arr. Alfred Moffat in *Old Masters for Young Players*, 3 OTT)

Bach, Carl Philipp Emanuel
- ● Marche, BWV Anh. 122 (arr. Constance Seely-Brown, in *Ten Little Classics* FIS)

Bach, Johann Sebastian, attr.
- ● Minuet 2 (Minuet in G Major), from *Notenbuch der Anna Magdalena Bach*, BWV Anh. 116 (arr. in *Suzuki Violin School, Revised Edition*, 1 ALF)
- ● Minuet 3 (Minuet in G Major) from *Notenbuch der Anna Magdalena Bach*, BWV Anh. 114 (Christian Petzold: attr. J.S. Bach and arr. in *Suzuki Violin School, Revised Edition*, 1 ALF)

Clarke, Jeremiah
- ▶ Minuet from *Choice Lessons for the Harpsichord or Spinet* (arr. Christine Donkin FHM)

Cofalik, Antoni, and Romuald Twardowski
At the Zoo BAR
- ● The Beavers (Die Biber)

Colledge, Katherine, and Hugh Colledge
Fast Forward B&H
- ▶ The Ceilidh
- ● Hornpipe

Shooting Stars B&H
- ▶ Five-a-Side
- ● Look Lively

De Fesch, Willem
- ● Esperanza (arr. Alfred Moffat in *Old Fiddle Pieces* OTT)

Donkin, Christine
Costume Party FHM
- ▶ The Dancer

Fall Fair FHM
- ▶ Fall Fair

Duke, David
- ▶ Motorcycles (in *The Encore Series for Violin & Piano*, 2 FHM)

Elgar, Edward
Six Very Easy Pieces in the First Position, op. 22 FAB; BOS
- ● Allegretto in G Major (no. 5)
- ▶ Allegro in C Major (no. 6)

Fleming, Robert
- ● Singer Man CMC

Girard, Anthony
- ● Le soleil luit pour tout le monde BIL

Handel, George Frideric
- ● Bourrée, from Sonata in F Major for Oboe and Basso Continuo, HWV 363 (arr. in *Suzuki Violin School, Revised Edition*, 2 ALF)

Haydn, Franz Joseph
- ▶ Minuet and Trio, from Divertimento in D Major for Baryton, Viola, and Cello, Hob. XI:34 (arr. FHM)

Kabalevsky, Dmitri
Twenty Pieces for Violin and Piano, op. 80 SCH; SIK
- ● Polka (no. 13)
- ▶ Skipping and Hopping (no. 8)

Losy, Johann Anton [Jan Antonín]
- ● Bourrée (arr. Ferenc Brodzsky in *Old Music for Violin* EMB)

Lumsden, Caroline, and Ben Attwood
Wizard's Potion PET
- ▶ Flash of Light'ning
- ● Strike It Lucky!

Mackay, Neil
Four Modern Dance Tunes S&B
- ● Rebecca
- ▶ Tango

Mozart, Wolfgang Amadeus
- ● Pantomime, from *Les petits riens*, K 10 (arr. Paul de Keyser and Fanny Waterman in *The Young Violinist's Repertoire*, 4 FAB)

Pracht, Robert
Twelve Easy Pieces, op. 12 BMC
- ▶ Hongrois (Hungarian)
  → observe repeat in Trio only
- ● Wandering

Schubert, Franz
- ▶ Waltz in D Major, D 420, no. 1 (arr. Kathleen Wood FHM)

Shostakovich, Dmitri
- ● Kleiner Marsch (arr. Konstantin Fortunatov in *Shostakovich: Albumstücke* PET)
- ▶ Hurdy-Gurdy (arr. Konstantin Fortunatov in *Shostakovich: Albumstücke* PET)

Weber, Carl Maria von
- ● Gypsy Dance (in *The Young Violinist's Repertoire*, 3 FAB)
- ● Hunters' Chorus, from *Der Freischütz* (in *Suzuki Violin School, Revised Edition*, 2 ALF)

Technical Requirements

Please see "Technical Requirements" on p. 11 for important information regarding this section of the examination.

Etudes

Candidates must prepare *two* technically contrasting etudes from the following list.

Bullets used to denote selections for examination purposes:
- ● one selection
- ▶ selection is found in *Violin Series, 2013 Edition: Violin Technique and Etudes Preparatory–4* FHM

Traditional
- ▶ Charlie Is My Darling FHM

Cohen, Mary
Scaley Monsters for Violin FAB
- ● Donkey Riding

Superstudies for Violin, 2 FAB
- ▶ Saturday Night Stomp

de Keyser, Paul
Violin Playtime Studies FAB
- ● German Folk-Song (no. 26)
- ● March (no. 29)
- ▶ Rowing on the Lake (no. 27)
- ● Trumpet Tune (no. 18)

Donkin, Christine
Get Fiddlin'! FHM
- ● Osoyoos (no. 12)
- ▶ Pancake Peak (no. 8)
  → play in 3rd position

Geringas, Yaakov
Shifting: Thirty Progressive Studies for Violinists FHM
- ● Country Dance (no. 17)
- ▶ Gym (no. 2)
  → play with given fingering
- ● Hide and Seek (no. 4)

Givens, Shirley
Adventures in Violinland, 3D GIV
- ● Spend Your Bow Wisely

Harris, Paul
Improve your Scales!, 1–2 FAB
- ● Arietta
- ● Greyhound

Improve your Scales!, 4 FAB
- ● Drifting
- ● Flamingo

Kinsey, Herbert
Elementary Progressive Studies, set 1 ABR
- ● *one* of nos. 9, 10, 12, 14, 16

Metz, Louis
Vioolmethode 2 B&V
- ● *one* of nos. 13, 21, 40

Milburn, Richard
- ▶ Listen to the Mockingbird (arr. Shirley Givens in *Adventures in Violinland*, 3D GIV)
  → play in 3rd position

Rhoda, Janice Tucker
The ABCs of Violin for The Absolute Beginner FIS
- ● Bobbing for Apples Jig (no. 77)

Romberg, Bernhard Heinrich
Twenty-seven Etudes for Strings GVT
- ▶ Sailing (arr. A. Baird Knechtel)

RT, Zav, arr.
Fiddleworks, 1 FHM
- ● Road to Lisdoonvarna

Sitt, Hans
Studies for Violin, op. 32, 1 FIS
- ● no. 2 *or* no. 5

Suzuki, Shin'ichi
Position Etudes, Revised Edition ALF
- ● Perpetual Motion in G Major, 3rd Position (with sixteenth-note variation, unaccompanied)

Wohlfahrt, Franz
Sixty Studies for Violin, op. 45, 1 SCH
- ▶ Study in F Major (no. 5)
- ● *one* of nos. 1, 2, 8, 9

Technical Tests

Please see "Technical Tests" on p. 11 for important information regarding this section of the examination.

Candidates must play all scales, arpeggios, and double stops from memory. Refer to *Violin Series, 2013 Edition: Violin Technique and Etudes Preparatory–4* FHM for required patterns.

Scales	Keys	Range	Tempo	Bowing
Major	G, A	2 octaves	♪ = 80	♫
Harmonic Minor	G, A			
Melodic Minor	G, A	1 octave start on open string	♩ = 88	♩♩
Major	F	1 octave	♪ = 80	♫
	D	1 octave in 3rd position start on A string	♩ = 100	𝅗𝅥
Arpeggios				
Major	G, A	2 octaves	♩ = 80	♩♩♩
Minor	G, A			
Major	F	1 octave	♩ = 80	♩♩♩
	D	1 octave in 3rd position start on A string	♩ = 60	♩
Double Stops*				
Exercise on A and E Strings			♩ = 80	𝅗𝅥

*See *Violin Series, 2013 Edition: Violin Technique and Etudes Preparatory–4* FHM.

Ear Tests

Clapback

Candidates will choose to either clap or tap the rhythm of a short melody after the examiner has played it *twice* on the piano.

Time Signatures	Approximate Length
2/4 3/4	four measures

Example only

1

2

Intervals

Candidates will be asked to identify the following intervals. The examiner will play each interval *once* in broken form on the piano.

or

Candidates may choose to sing or hum the following intervals. The examiner will play the first note *once* on the piano.

Above a Given Note
major 3rd
perfect 5th

Playback

Candidates will be asked to play back a melody on the violin, based on the first five notes of a major scale. The melody may contain one or more leaps of a 3rd. The examiner will name the key, play the tonic triad *once*, and play the melody *twice* on the piano.

Beginning Note	Keys	Approximate Length
tonic or dominant	G, D, A major	five notes

Example only

1

2

Grade 3

Candidates in Grade 3 should be able to use a variety of bow strokes appropriately, including *staccato*, *martelé*, and *detaché*. Secure intonation in 1st, 2nd, and 3rd positions is required, including the ability to shift between positions with accuracy and fluency. The development of vibrato is encouraged at this level.

Grade 3 Requirements	Marks
Repertoire	**60**
one selection from List A	18
one selection from List B	18
one selection from List C	18
Memory (2 marks per repertoire selection)	6
Technical Requirements	**20**
Etudes: *two* etudes from the *Syllabus* list	10
Technical Tests	10
– scales	
– arpeggios	
– double stops	
Ear Tests	**10**
Clapback	3
Intervals	3
Playback	4
Sight Reading	**10**
Playing	7
Clapping	3
Total possible marks (pass = 60)	**100**
Theory Co-requisite	
None	

Repertoire

Please see "Examination Repertoire" on p. 9 for important information regarding this section of the examination.

Candidates must prepare *three* contrasting selections by three different composers, *one* from List A, *one* from List B, and *one* from List C.

Bullets used to denote selections for examination purposes:

- ● one selection
- ▶ selection is found in *Violin Series, 2013 Edition: Violin Repertoire 3* FHM

List A
Repertoire in Baroque and Classical Styles

Albrechtsberger, Johann Georg
- ▶ Minuetto and Trio in D Major, from Symphony No. 3 in D Major (arr. Paul Jenkins FHM)

Arne, Thomas A.
- ● Melodie in G Major (arr. Alfred Moffat in *Old Masters for Young Players*, 1 OTT)

Bach, Johann Sebastian, attr.
- ● Minuet, from *Notenbuch der Anna Magdalena Bach*, BWV Anh. 114 (Christian Petzold: attr. J.S. Bach and arr. in *Suzuki Violin School, Revised Edition*, 3 ALF)
- ▶ Musette, from *Notenbuch der Anna Magdalena Bach*, BWV Anh. 126 (arr. Kathleen Wood FHM)

Becker, Jean
- ● Gavotte (in *Suzuki Violin School, Revised Edition*, 3 ALF)

Beethoven, Ludwig van
- ● Minuet in G Major, from *Sechs Menuette*, WoO 10, no. 2 (arr. in *Suzuki Violin School, Revised Edition*, 2 ALF)

Diabelli, Anton
Sonatina, op. 163, no. 4
- ▶ 2nd movement: Andante cantabile (arr. Kathleen Wood FHM)

Gossec, François-Joseph
- ● Gavotte (in *Suzuki Violin School, Revised Edition*, 1 ALF)

Hasse, Johann Adolph
Two Dances (arr. Alfred Moffat, in *Old Masters for Young Players*, 1 OTT)
- ● Bourrée *and* Menuett

Küchler, Ferdinand
Concertino in G Major, op. 11 BOS
- ▶ 1st movement

Lully, Jean-Baptiste
- ● Gavotte (in *Suzuki Violin School, Revised Edition*, 2 ALF)

Martini, Giovanni Battista
- ● Gavotte (in *Suzuki Violin School, Revised Edition*, 3 ALF)

Montéclair, Michel Pignolet de
- ● Two Minuets (in *Position Pieces for Violin and Piano*, 2 FAB)

Pepusch, Johann Christoph
- ● Theatermusik (arr. Alfred Moffat in *Old Fiddle Pieces* OTT)

Sammartini, Giuseppe
- ● Mouvement d'une Sérénade (arr. Alfred Moffat in *Old Fiddle Pieces* OTT)

Steibelt, Daniel
- ● Divertimento (arr. Alfred Moffat, in *Old Fiddle Pieces* OTT; *The Young Violinist's Repertoire,* 2 FAB)

Telemann, Georg Philipp
Sonatina in F Major, TWV 41:F1
- ▶ 3rd movement: Presto (arr. Kathleen Wood FHM)

Mendelssohn, Ludwig
Miniatures: Fifteen Pieces for Violin, op. 62 BOS
- ● Cavatina (no. 4)
- ● Little Waltz (no. 2)

Paganini, Niccolò
- ● Theme, from *Witches' Dance* (arr. in *Suzuki Violin School, Revised Edition,* 2 ALF)

Schumann, Robert
- ● The Two Grenadiers, op. 49, no. 1 (arr. in *Suzuki Violin School, Revised Edition,* 2 ALF)

Tchaikovsky, Pyotr Il'yich
- ● Sharmanka (in *The Young Violinist's Repertoire,* 2 FAB)

List B
Traditional and Romantic Repertoire

Anonymous
- ● Untitled Reel 2 (arr. John Beckwith, in *Eight Miniatures from the Allen Ash Manuscript* FHM)

Traditional
- ▶ Nouvelle agréable (arr. Christine Donkin FHM)
  → play with fingering indicated
- ▶ Skye Boat Song (arr. Hugh J. McLean FHM)
  → play in 3rd position

Alard, Jean-Delphin
- ▶ Nocturne (In the Second Position) FHM
  → play in 2nd position

Baklanova, Nathalia
Acht leichte Stücke für Violine und Klavier PET
- ▶ Mazurka (no. 4) (in *The Young Violinist's Repertoire,* 3 FAB)
  → observe repeat mm. 33 to 40
- ● Romance (no. 3)

Blachford, Frank
- ▶ Minor Mode FHM

Brahms, Johannes
- ● Waltz, from *Walzer,* op. 39, no. 15 (arr. in *Suzuki Violin School, Revised Edition,* 2 ALF)

Carse, Adam
Fiddle Fancies S&B
- ● Waltz Steps

Dvořák, Antonín
- ● From "Songs My Mother Taught Me," op. 55, no. 4 (in *The Young Violinist's Repertoire,* 2 FAB)

Grieg, Edvard
- ▶ Wedding Tune, op. 17, no. 24 (arr. Kathleen Wood FHM)
  → play in 2nd position

Méhul, Etienne
- ● Romance (arr. Alfred Moffat in *Old Fiddle Pieces* OTT)

List C
Repertoire Composed After 1930

Archer, Violet
Twelve Miniatures WAT; CMC
- ● Joyous

Chase, Bruce
Fiddle & Fun in First Position HAL
- ▶ Gabby Ghost

Colledge, Katherine, and Hugh Colledge
Shooting Stars B&H
- ▶ Cossacks
- ▶ Moto perpetuo

Coulthard, Jean
- ▶ A Sad Waltz (in *The Encore Series for Violin & Piano,* 3 FHM)
- ● Under the Sea (in *The Encore Series for Violin & Piano,* 4 FHM)

Donkin, Christine
Fall Fair FHM
- ▶ The Farmers' Market
- ● Midway Ride

Duke, David
- ● Pibroch (in *The Encore Series for Violin & Piano,* 2 FHM)

Fiala, George
- ▶ Wallaby's Lullaby, op. 5 BER

Fleming, Robert
- ● Berceuse CMC
- ● Whistler's Tune CMC

Kabalevsky, Dmitri
Twenty Pieces for Violin and Piano, op. 80 SCH; SIK
- ▶ On Holiday (no. 15)

Khachaturian, Aram
- ● The Little Horse (in *Position Pieces for Violin and Piano,* 3 FAB)

Kroll, William
Three Violin Pieces in the First Position SCH
- ▶ Donkey Doodle (in *Solos for Young Violinists*, 1 ALF)

Lumsden, Caroline, and Ben Atwood
Wizard's Potion PET
- ● Grab the Slippery Toad!

Norton, Christopher
Microjazz Violin Collection, 2 B&H
- ● A Dramatic Episode
- ● Fly Away

Persichetti, Vincent
Masques, op. 99 EVO
- ● Masque No. 1

Pracht, Robert
Twelve Easy Pieces, op. 12 BMC
- ● Perpetuum Mobile
- ● Tarantella

Shostakovich, Dmitri
- ▶ The Clockwork Doll, from *Children's Notebook*, op. 69 (arr. Konstantin Fortunatov, in *Shostakovich: Albumstücke* PET)

Wilson, Peter
Space Stringpops FAB
- ● Space Walk

Technical Requirements

Please see "Technical Requirements" on p. 11 for important information regarding this section of the examination.

Etudes

Candidates must prepare *two* technically contrasting etudes from the following list.

Bullets used to denote selections for examination purposes:
- ● one selection
- ▶ selection is found in *Violin Series, 2013 Edition: Violin Technique and Etudes Preparatory–4* FHM

Cohen, Mary
Superstudies for Violin, 2 FAB
- ● Fivepenny Waltz (no. 8)
- ● Hot Chocolate Treat (no. 3)
- ● The Snake-Charmer's Lament (no. 7)
- ▶ The Whirly Bird and the Hen (no. 9)

de Keyser, Paul
Violin Playtime Studies FAB
- ● Allegro Brillante (no. 30)

Donkin, Christine
Get Fiddlin'! FHM
- ● Kananaskis (no. 22)
- ● Mosquito Creek (no. 20)
- ● Simonette River (no. 16)
- ● Wild Horse (no. 10)

Entezami, Ramin
Melodious Etudes in First Position FIS
- ▶ The Fellow (no. 31)

Geringas, Yaakov
Shifting: Thirty Progressive Studies for Violinists FHM
- ● Aim and Shoot (no. 8)
- ● Cradle Song (no. 6)
- ▶ The First Skating Lesson (no. 5)
- ● King Counter (no. 7)
- ● Round Dance (no. 3)
- ● Sadness (no. 18)
- ● Tag (no. 11)
- ● Up and Down the Ladder (no. 1)

Givens, Shirley
Adventures in Violinland, 3D GIV
- ▶ Who Has Seen the Wind?
  → play in 3rd position

Kayser, Heinrich Ernst
Elementary and Progressive Studies for the Violin, op. 20 SCH; FIS
- ● *one* of nos. 1, 2, 3

Kinsey, Herbert
Elementary Progressive Studies, set 1 ABR
- ● no. 11 *or* no. 18

Mackay, Neil
Position Changing for the Violin OUP
- ▶ The Fair Isle (no. 2)
- ● Tyrolean Air (no. 18)

Metz, Louis
Vioolmethode, 3 B&V
- ● no. 8

Rapoport, Katharine
- ▶ Kites FHM
  → play in 2nd position

Sitt, Hans
Studies for the Violin, op. 32, 1 FIS
- ● no. 3 *or* no. 4

Trott, Josephine
Melodious Double Stops, 1 SCH
- ● *one* of nos. 1, 2, 4, 6, 7, 8

Wohlfahrt, Franz
Forty Elementary Studies, op. 54 FIS; SCH; PET
- ● no. 9 *or* no. 35

Sixty Studies for Violin, op. 45, 1 SCH
- ▶ Study in G Major (no. 4)
- ● *one* of nos. 6, 14, 16, 20

Sixty Studies for Violin, op. 45, 2 SCH
- ▶ Study in B flat Major (no. 37)

Technical Tests

Please see "Technical Tests" on p. 11 for important information regarding this section of the examination.

Candidates must play all scales, arpeggios, and double stops from memory. Refer to *Violin Series, 2013 Edition: Violin Technique and Etudes Preparatory–4* FHM for required patterns.

Scales	Keys	Range	Tempo	Bowing
Major	B♭, C, D	2 octaves	♪ = 100	
Harmonic and Melodic Minor	C, D			
Major	F	1 octave in 2nd position	♩ = 60	
Harmonic and Melodic Minor	F			
Chromatic	on D	1 octave start on open string	♩ = 66	
Arpeggios				
Major	B♭, C, D	2 octaves	♩ = 88	
Minor	C, D			
Major	F	1 octave in 2nd position	♩ = 60	
Minor	F			
Double Stops*				
Exercise on D and A Strings			♩ = 60	

*See *Violin Series, 2013 Edition: Violin Technique and Etudes Preparatory–4* FHM.

Ear Tests

Clapback

Candidates will choose to either clap or tap the rhythm of a short melody after the examiner has played it *twice* on the piano.

Time Signatures	Approximate Length
2/4 3/4 4/4	four measures

Example only

1

2

Intervals

Candidates will be asked to identify the following intervals. The examiner will play each interval *once* in broken form on the piano.
or
Candidates may choose to sing or hum the following intervals. The examiner will play the first note *once* on the piano.

Above a Given Note	Below a Given Note
major 3rd	minor 3rd
perfect 5th	perfect 5th
perfect octave	

Playback

Candidates will be asked to play back a melody on the violin, based on the first five notes of a major scale. The melody may contain leaps of a 3rd and/or a 5th. The examiner will name the key, play the tonic triad *once*, and play the melody *twice* on the piano.

Beginning Note	Keys	Approximate Length
tonic, mediant, or dominant	G, D, A major	five to eight notes

Example only

1

2

Sight Reading

Playing

Candidates will be asked to play a short melody at sight. This may contain dynamics (***p***, ***mp***, ***mf***, ***f***, *dim.*, *cresc.*), symbols (𝄐), articulation, and bowing indications (two-note *legato* or *staccato* slurs).

Difficulty	Time Signatures	Keys	Positions	Approximate Length
Grade 1 repertoire	$\frac{3}{4}$ $\frac{4}{4}$	G, D, A major	1st	eight to twelve measures

Clapping

Candidates will be asked to clap or tap a rhythm. A steady pulse and rhythmic precision are expected.

Time Signatures	Approximate Length
$\frac{3}{4}$ $\frac{4}{4}$	four measures

Example only

Grade 4

Candidates in Grade 4 should be able to use a variety of bow strokes appropriately, including brush strokes, *staccato*, *martelé*, and *detaché*. Secure intonation in 1st to 4th positions is expected, including the ability to shift between positions with accuracy and fluency. Some vibrato is expected at this level.

Grade 4 Requirements	Marks
Repertoire	**60**
one selection from List A	18
one selection from List B	18
one selection from List C	18
Memory (2 marks per repertoire selection)	6
Technical Requirements	**20**
Etudes: *two* etudes from the *Syllabus* list	10
Technical Tests	10
– scales	
– arpeggios	
– double stops	
Ear Tests	**10**
Clapback	3
Intervals	3
Playback	4
Sight Reading	**10**
Playing	7
Clapping	3
Total possible marks (pass = 60)	**100**
Theory Co-requisite	
None	

Repertoire

Please see "Examination Repertoire" on p. 9 for important information regarding this section of the examination.

Candidates must prepare *three* contrasting selections by three different composers: *one* from List A, *one* from List B, and *one* from List C.

Bullets used to denote selections for examination purposes:

- ● one selection
- ▶ selection is found in *Violin Series, 2013 Edition: Violin Repertoire 4* FHM

List A
Concertos, Sonatinas, and Fantasias

Baklanova, Natalya Vladimirovna
Acht leichte Stücke für Violine und Klavier PET
- ● Concertino (no. 8)

Dancla, Charles
Douze fantasies sur motifs favouris, op. 86 FIS
- ● Le cor des Alpes–Valse du Freischütz (no. 11)
- ● Fleuve du Tage (no. 8)
- ● Rédowa de Wallerstein (no. 3)

Küchler, Ferdinand
Concertino in D Major, op. 12 BOS
- ● 1st *or* 3rd movement

Concertino in the Style of Antonio Vivaldi, op. 15 BOS; (in *Solos for Young Violinists*, 1 ALF)
- ● 1st movement
- ▶ 3rd movement

Millies, Hans Mollenhauer
Concertino in the Style of W.A. Mozart (abridged) NOV
- ▶ 1st movement

Mollenhauer, Eduard
- ▶ The Infant Paganini: Fantasia FIS

Perlman, George
Concertino in A Minor (in *Fun with Solos* CHD)
- ● 3rd movement

Portnoff, Leo
Russian Fantasias BOS
- ● Russian Fantasia No. 2 in D Minor
- ● Russian Fantasia No. 3 in A Minor

Rieding, Oskar
Concerto in B Minor, op. 35 BAR; BOS
- ● 1st movement
- ▶ 3rd movement

Concerto in D Major, op. 36 BOS
- ● 3rd movement

Concerto in G Major, op. 34 BOS
- ● 1st movement

Ruegger, Charlotte
- ● Concertante in G Major FIS

Steibelt, Daniel
Sonatine, op. 33, no. 1
- ▶ 1st movement

List B
Repertoire in Baroque Style

Anonymous
- ▶ Bourrée, from Leopold Mozart, *Notenbuch für Wolfgang* (arr. Kathleen Wood FHM)

Aubert, Jacques
- ● Two Minuets (arr. Elma Doflein and Erich Doflein in *Musik für Violine und Klavier,* 2 OTT)

Bach, Johann Sebastian
- ● Gavotte in G Minor (Gavotte en rondeau) from Suite in G Minor for Harpsichord, BWV 822, arr. in *Suzuki Violin School, Revised Edition,* 3 ALF)
- ▶ Giguetta from *Sarabande con Partite,* BWV 990, XVI: L'ultima Partita o Giguetta (arr. Constance Seely-Brown in *Ten Little Classics* FIS and *Solos for Young Violinists,* 1 ALF)

Corelli, Arcangelo
Sonata in F Major, op. 5, no. 10
- ▶ 4th movement: Gavotta (arr. Kathleen Wood FHM)

Handel, George Frideric
- ● Sarabande from Concerto in G Minor for oboe, strings, and basso continuo, HWV 287 (arr. Harold Edwin Darke ABR)
- ▶ Sarabande from Keyboard Suite in D Minor, HWV 447 (arr. Christine Gale FHM)

Lully, Jean-Baptiste
- ● Gavotte and Musette (arr. Alfred Moffat, in *Old Masters for Young Players,* 1 OTT)

Telemann, Georg Philipp
Sonatina No. 2 in B flat Major, TWV 41:B2
- ● Presto (in *Baroque Violin Pieces,* 2 ABR)

Thomas, Ambroise
- ● Gavotte from *Mignon* (arr. in *Suzuki Violin School, Revised Edition,* 2 ALF)

List C
Concert Repertoire

Traditional
- ● Bán Chnoic Eireann O (arr. T.C. Kelly in *Irish Tunes,* 2 OSS)
- ● The Lark in the Clear Air (arr. T.C. Kelly in *Irish Tunes,* 2 OSS)

Baklanova, Natalya Vladimirovna
Acht leichte Stücke für Violine und Klavier PET
- ● Allegro (no. 6)
- ▶ Fast Dance (Reigen) (no. 2) (in *The Young Violinist's Repertoire,* 3 FAB)

Barns, Ethel
- ▶ Le faun (in *Music for Strings* LEE)

Bennett, Richard Rodney
Up Bow, Down Bow NOV
- ▶ Merry-Go-Round

Bloch, József
Vier leichte Stücke, op. 36 SDM
- ● Historiette (no. 4)

Boccherini, Luigi
- ● Minuet (in *Suzuki Violin School, Revised Edition,* 2 ALF)

Bouchard, Rémi
Suite for Violin and Piano BMC
- ● String Along

Dancla, Charles
Petite école de la mélodie, op. 123, 1 OTT
- ● Polka (no. 6)

Dvořák, Antonín
- ● Humoresque (from *Humoresques for Piano,* op. 101, no. 7, arr. in *Suzuki Violin School, Revised Edition,* 3 ALF)

Ethridge, Jean
- ● Two Blues (in *The Encore Series for Violin & Piano,* 3 FHM)

Hook, James
- ● My Heart Is Devoted, Dear Mary, to Thee (arr. John Beckwith, in *Eight Miniatures from the Allen Ash Manuscript* FHM)

Kabalevsky, Dmitri
Twenty Pieces for Violin and Piano, op. 80 SCH; SIK
- ● Ping Pong (no. 18)
- ▶ Summer Song (no. 16)

Mendelssohn, Felix
- ● Allegro non troppo, from *Sechs Kinderstücke,* op. 72, no. 1 (arr. István Nagy in *Leichte Stücke für Violine und Klavier* UNI)

Mendelssohn, Ludwig
Miniatures: Fifteen Pieces for Violin, op. 62 BOS
- ● Conte sérieux (no. 6)
- ● Mosquito Dance (no. 5) (in *Solos for Young Violinists,* 1 ALF)
- ▶ Soldatenmarsch (Soldier's March) (no. 3)

Nakada, Yoshinao
Japanese Festival
- ▶ The Song of Twilight (in *Position Pieces for Violin and Piano* PRE)
  → play in 4th position

Nelson, Sheila M.
Moving Up Again B&H
- ● Caprice
- ● Moto Perpetuo

Palaschko, Johannes
Ten Easy Pieces, op. 65
- ● March of the Pirates (no. 5)

Schumann, Robert
- ▶ Knecht Ruprecht (Knight Rupert) from *Album für die Jugend*, op. 68 (arr. FHM)

Spies, Ernst
Sechs Stücke, op. 45 OTT
- ● Menuetto (no. 5) FIS

Rieding, Oskar
Vier Leichte Vortragsstücke, op. 23 BUT
- ● Ziguernermarsch (no. 2) BOS

Tchaikovsky, Pyotr Il'yich
- ▶ Danse napolitaine (Neapolitan Dance) from *Swan Lake*, op. 20 (arr. FHM)

Trott, Josephine
- ● The Puppet Show, op. 5, no. 1 (in *Solos for Young Violinists*, 1 ALF)

Vaughan Williams, Ralph
Six Studies in English Folk-Song S&B
- ● Andante Tranquillo (no. 6)

Technical Requirements

Please see "Technical Requirements" on p. 11 for important information regarding this section of the examination.

Etudes

Candidates must prepare *two* technically contrasting etudes from the following list.

Bullets used to denote selections for examination purposes:
- ● one selection
- ▶ selection is found in *Violin Series, 2013 Edition: Violin Technique and Etudes Preparatory—4* FHM

Cohen, Mary
Technique Takes Off!, 2 FAB
- ● Magic Carpet Ride (no. 11)
- ▶ The Mill Wheel (no. 4)

Entezami, Ramin
Melodious Etudes in First Position FIS
- ▶ The Happy Wire-Haired Dachshund (no. 60)
  → with repeat
- ● Little Boat on the Sea (no. 59)

Geringas, Yaakov
Shifting: Thirty Progressive Studies for Violinists FHM
- ● Agitation (no. 19)
- ● At the Skating Rink (no. 28)
- ● Barcarolle (no. 30)
- ▶ Grasshopper (no. 10)
- ● Hop Scotch (no. 15)
- ● Lost in the Woods (no. 22)
- ● March (no. 20)
- ● Old Dance (no. 12)
- ▶ Playing Ball (no. 9)
- ● A Pleasant Day (no. 21)
- ● Scherzino (no. 25)
- ● Tongue Twister (no. 29)

Grissen, Carl
Learn With Tunes, 3 WIL
- ● Lesson 17 (no. 3)
- ● Lesson 19 (no. 4)

Kayser, Heinrich Ernst
Elementary and Progressive Studies for the Violin, op. 20 SCH; FIS
- ● no. 4 *or* no. 13

Kinnard, Kathryn Bird
Easy Songs for Shifting in the First Five Positions ALF
- ● Gypsy Dance
- ▶ Inch Worm
  → play with given fingering
- ● Popsicles

Kinsey, Herbert
Elementary Progressive Studies, 2 ABR
- ● Set 1, no. 19
- ● Set 2, no. 7

Panofka, Heinrich
- ● no. 10 *or* no. 26 (in *Studies in Lyricism for Violin* FIS)

RT, Zav, arr.
Fiddleworks, 3 FHM
- ▶ Ostinelli's Reel

Sitt, Hans
Studies for the Violin, op. 32, 1 FIS
- ● no. 6 *or* no. 7

Trott, Josephine
Melodious Double Stops, 1 SCH
- ▶ Melodious Double Stops (no. 9)
- ● no. 5

Wohlfahrt, Franz
Forty Elementary Studies, op. 54 FIS; SCH; PET
- ● no. 8

Sixty Studies for Violin, op. 45, 1 SCH
- ▶ Study in F Major (no. 6)

Sixty Studies for Violin, op. 45, 2 SCH
- ● *one* of nos. 18, 31–37 (omit articulations)

Technical Tests

Please see “Technical Tests” on p. 11 for important information regarding this section of the examination.

Candidates must play all scales, arpeggios, and double stops from memory. Refer to *Violin Series, 2013 Edition: Violin Technique and Etudes Preparatory–4* FHM for required patterns.

Scales	Keys	Range	Tempo	Bowing
Major	A♭, B, E♭	2 octaves	♩ = 60	
Harmonic and Melodic Minor	B, E♭			
Major	E	1 octave in 4th position	♩ = 84	
Harmonic and Melodic Minor	E			
Major	B	1 octave on A string	♩ = 84	
Chromatic	on E	1 octave start on D string	♩ = 84	
Arpeggios				
Major	A♭, B, E♭	2 octaves	♩ = 96	
Minor	B, E♭			
Major	E	1 octave in 4th position	♩ = 84	
Minor	E			
Dominant 7th of Major Keys	G (starting on D), A (starting on E)	1 octave start on D string	♩ = 84	
Diminished 7th of Minor Keys	B♭ (starting on A♮), E♭ (starting on D♮)	1 octave start on open string	♩ = 84	
Double Stops				
Major in Broken 6ths	E♭	1 octave	♩ = 60	

Ear Tests

Clapback

Candidates will choose to either clap or tap the rhythm of a short melody after the examiner has played it *twice* on the piano.

Time Signatures	Approximate Length
2/4 6/8	three to four measures

Example only

1

2

Intervals

Candidates will be asked to identify the following intervals. The examiner will play each interval *once* in broken form on the piano.

or

Candidates may choose to sing or hum the following intervals. The examiner will play the first note *once* on the piano.

Above a Given Note	Below a Given Note
major and minor 3rds	minor 3rd
perfect 4th	
perfect 5th	perfect 5th
perfect octave	perfect octave

Playback

Candidates will be asked to play back a melody, based on the first five notes of a major scale, on the violin. The examiner will name the key, play the tonic triad *once,* and play the melody *twice* on the piano.

Beginning Note	Keys	Approximate Length
tonic, mediant, or dominant	C, G, D, A major	six notes

Example only

Sight Reading

Playing

Candidates will be asked to play a short melody at sight. New features introduced at Grade 4 may include accidentals, *tenuto* markings, and dynamic indications from ***pp*** to ***ff***.

Difficulty	Time Signatures	Keys	Positions	Approximate Length
Grade 2 repertoire	2/4 3/4 4/4	C, F, G, D major	1st	eight to twelve measures

Clapping

Candidates will be asked to clap or tap the rhythm of a melody. A steady pulse and rhythmic precision are expected.

Time Signatures	Approximate Length
3/4 4/4	four measures

Example only

Grade 5

Candidates in Grade 5 should have a well-developed brush stroke and beginning *collé* and *spiccato* strokes. Secure intonation in 1st to 5th positions is expected, including the ability to shift between positions with accuracy and fluency. Candidates should be able to produce vibrato consistently with all fingers.

Grade 5 Requirements	Marks
Repertoire	**60**
one selection from List A	17
one selection from List B	20
one selection from List C	17
Memory (3 marks each for List A and List C)	6
Technical Requirements	**20**
Etudes: *two* etudes from the *Syllabus* list	10
Technical Tests	10
– scales	
– arpeggios	
Ear Tests	**10**
Clapback	3
Intervals	3
Playback	4
Sight Reading	**10**
Playing	7
Clapping	3
Total possible marks (pass = 60)	**100**
Theory Co-requisite	
Basic Rudiments	

Repertoire

Please see "Examination Repertoire" on p. 9 for important information regarding this section of the examination.

Candidates must prepare *three* contrasting selections by three different composers: *one* from List A, *one* from List B, and *one* from List C.

Bullets used to denote selections for examination purposes:

- ● one selection
- ▶ selection is found in *Violin Series, 2013 Edition: Violin Repertoire 5* FHM

List A
Concertos, *Airs variés,* and Fantasias

Bacewicz, Grażyna
Concertino PWM
- ▶ 1st movement

Bériot, Charles-Auguste de
- ● Air varié No. 14 in G Major (in *Solos for Young Violinists,* 2 ALF)

Dancla, Charles
Airs variés, op. 89 OTT; FIS; SCH
- ● Air varié on a Theme by Pacini (no. 1)

Douze fantasies sur motifs favouris, op. 86 FIS
- ● La Cenerentola (no. 7)
- ● Donna del Lago–Air suisse (no. 4)
- ● Les noces de Figaro–Le crociato (no. 10)
- ▶ Plaisir d'amour (no. 12)
- ● Les Puritains (no. 9)

Huber, Adolf
Concertino in G Major, op. 6, no. 2 FIS
- ● 1st movement (to end of p. 1 of violin part)

Concertino in G Major, op. 8, no. 4 FIS
- ● complete

Járdányi, Pál
- ● Concertino EMB

Portnoff, Leo
Russian Fantasias BOS
- ● Russian Fantasia No. 1 in A Minor BOS

Rieding, Oskar
- ▶ Air varié, op. 23, no. 3 BOS

Seitz, Friedrich
Concerto No. 2 in G Major, op. 13 BOS; SCH (in *Suzuki Violin School, Revised Edition,* 4 ALF)
- ● 3rd movement

Concerto No. 5 in D Major, op. 22 BOS; SCH (in *Suzuki Violin School, Revised Edition,* 4 ALF)
- ● 1st movement

List B
Sonatas and Sonatinas

Corelli, Arcangelo
12 Sonate, op. 5 BAR; OTT
Sonata No. 7 in D Minor (arr. István Homolya EMB)
- ● 1st movement: Preludio *and* 2nd movement: Corrente
- ● 3rd movement: Sarabanda *and* 4th movement: Giga

Sonata No. 8 in E Minor
- ● 1st movement: Preludio *and* 2nd movement: Allemanda
- ● 3rd movement: Sarabanda *and* 4th movement: Giga

Sonata No. 9 in A Major
- ● 1st movement: Preludio *and* 2nd movement: Giga

Sonata No. 11 in E Major
- ● 1st movement: Preludio *and* 2nd movement: Allegro

De Fesch, William
Sonata in G Major, op. 8, no. 4
- ● Largo *and* Allemanda (in *Baroque Violin Pieces,* 2 ABR)

Pepusch, Johann Christoph
Six Sonatas, op. 1 OTT
Sonata No. 3 in G Major (arr. René Colwell OTT)
- ● 1st movement: Adagio *and* 2nd movement: Allegro
- ● 3rd movement: Adagio *and* 4th movement: Allegro

Sonata No. 5 in G Major (arr. Siegfried Pritsche PET; arr. René Colwell OTT)
- ● 1st movement: Adagio *and* 2nd movement: Allegro
- ● 3rd movement: Adagio *and* 4th movement: Allegro

Scarlatti, Domenico
Sonata No. 2 in E Minor, K 81 (in *5 Sonate per violino e basso continuo* EMB)
- ● 3rd movement: Grave *and* 4th movement: Allegro

Sonata No. 5 in G Major, K 91 (in *5 Sonate per violino e basso continuo* EMB)
- ● 3rd movement: Grave *and* 4th movement: Allegro

Telemann, Georg Philipp
Sei Sonatine per Violino e Cembalo EMB
Sonata in E Major, TWV 41: E1
- ▶ 1st movement: Affettuoso–Siciliano *and* 4th movement: Allegro (arr. Kathleen Wood FHM)
  → with all repeats

Vanhal, Johann Baptist
Kurz und leichte Klavierstücke begleitet mit einer Violine
Sonata No. 1 (in *Easy Classical Sonatas for Violin and Piano* EMB)
- ▶ 1st movement: Cadenza-Siciliano *and* 2nd movement: Allegretto

Weber, Carl Maria von
Six sonates progressives pour le pianoforte avec violon obligé, op. 10b HEN
Sonata No. 2
- ▶ 3rd movement: Air Polonais

List C
Concert Repertoire

Traditional
- ▶ Ukrainian Folk Song (arr. Michael Conway Baker)

Adaskin, Murray
- ● Quiet Song CMC

Bach, Johann Sebastian
- ● Bourrée from Suite for Cello No. 3 in C Major, BWV 1009 (arr. in *Suzuki Violin School, Revised Edition,* 3 ALF)

Blachford, Frank
- ▶ Mazurka FHM

Bohm, Carl
- ● Moto Perpetuo (from the "*Third Suite*" BMC)

Coulthard, Jean
- ● On the March BER; CMC
- ● Music on a Hebridean Folk Song (in *The Encore Series for Violin & Piano,* 5 FHM)

Dolin, Samuel
- ▶ Little Sombrero BER; CMC

Donkin, Christine
Fall Fair FHM
- ● Barn Dance

Duke, David
- ▶ Abracadabra (for Kathy Rapoport) (in *The Encore Series for Violin & Piano,* 4 FHM)

Ethridge, Jean
- ▶ Fairy Tale (in *The Encore Series for Violin & Piano,* 6 FHM)
- ● Gig (in *The Encore Series for Violin & Piano,* 5 FHM)
- ● Reverie (in *The Encore Series for Violin & Piano,* 4 FHM)

Gluck, Christoph Willibald
- ▶ Musette and Air de ballet, from *Armide* (arr. Kathleen Wood FHM)

Grieg, Edvard
- ▶ Waltz from *Lyric Pieces* op. 12, no. 2 (arr. Hans Sitt) (in *Solos for the Violin Player* HAL; SCH)
  → with repeat

Hadjiev, Parashkev
- ▶ Rondino (in *The Young Violinist's Repertoire,* 4 FAB)

Heins, Donald
- ● Country Dance PRE

Jaque, Rhené
- ● Daussila BER
- ● Mouvement perpétuel IND

Jenkinson, Ezra
- ● Elfentanz (Danse des sylphes) BOS; (in *Solos for Young Violinists,* 1 ALF)

Kreisler, Fritz
Four Pieces for Violin and Piano FIS; MAS
- ▶ Toy Soldiers' March

Mendelssohn, Ludwig
Miniatures: Fifteen Pieces for Violin, op. 62 BOS
- ● Polonaise (no. 1)

Norton, Christopher
Microjazz Violin Collection, 2 B&H
- ● Snow Dance

Shostakovich, Dmitri
- ▶ Dance from *Dances of the Dolls* (arr. Konstantin Fortunatov, in *Shostakovich: Albumstücke* PET)

Vaughan Williams, Ralph
Six Studies in English Folk-Song S&B
- ▶ Allegro Vivace (no. 6)

Woof, Rowsby
- ● Hornpipe (in *Fiddler's Choice*, 6 ABR)

Technical Requirements

Please see "Technical Requirements" on p. 11 for important information regarding this section of the examination.

Etudes

Candidates must prepare *two* technically contrasting etudes from the following list.

Bullets used to denote selections for examination purposes:
- ● one selection
- ▶ selection is found in *Violin Series, 2013 Edition: Violin Etudes and Technique 5–8* FHM

Cohen, Mary
Technique Takes Off!, FAB
- ▶ The Bee's Knees! (no. 12)
  - → omit all repeats
- ● Dragon Dance (no. 7)
- ● Looping the Loop (no. 4)

Concone, Giuseppe
- ● Andante Cantabile (no. 13) (in *Studies in Lyricism for Violin* FIS)

Geringas, Yaakov
Shifting: Thirty Progressive Studies for Violinists FHM
- ▶ Ballet Variation (no. 23)
- ● Love My Mum (no. 26)

Griesdale, Susan
Soundplay: Eight Character Pieces GRI
- ▶ Jolly Rondo

Grissen, Carl
Learn With Tunes, 3 WIL
- ● Lesson 21 (no. 6)

Kayser, Heinrich Ernst
Elementary and Progressive Studies for the Violin, op. 20 SCH; FIS
- ▶ Study in G Major (no. 13)
- ● *one* of nos. 5, 6, 8, 19

Sitt, Hans
Studies for the Violin, op. 32, 1 FIS
- ▶ Study in C Major (no. 12)
- ● *one* of nos. 8–11

Trott, Josephine
Melodious Double Stops, 1 SCH
- ▶ Melodious Double Stops (no. 11)
- ● *one* of nos. 10, 12, 13, 15, 16, 18

Wohlfahrt, Franz
Fifty Easy Melodic Studies, op. 74, 1 FIS
- ● no. 21

Fifty Easy Melodic Studies, op. 74, 2 FIS
- ▶ no. 29

Forty Elementary Studies, op. 54 SCH; PET
- ● no. 18

Sixty Studies for Violin, op. 45, 2 SCH; FIS
- ▶ Study in C Major (no. 42)
- ● no. 44 *or* no. 45

Technical Tests

Please see "Technical Tests" on p. 11 for important information regarding this section of the examination.

Candidates must play all scales, arpeggios, and double stops from memory. Refer to *Violin Series, 2013 Edition: Violin Technique and Etudes 5–8* FHM for required patterns.

Scales	Keys	Range	Tempo	Bowing
Major	G	3 octaves	♩ = 76	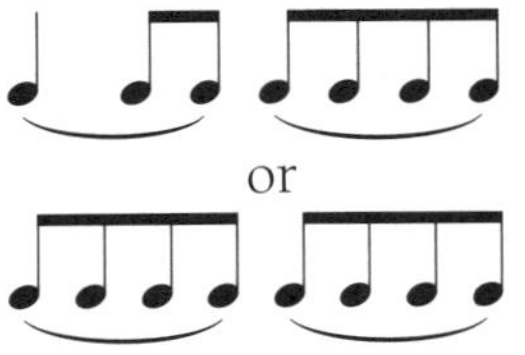
Major	A♭, E, F	2 octaves	♩ = 88	
Harmonic and Melodic Minor	G♯, E, F			
Major	C	1 octave on A string	♩ = 84	
Chromatic	on G, on A	2 octaves	♩ = 76	
Arpeggios				
Major	A♭, E, F	2 octaves	♩ = 120	
Minor	G♯, E, F			
Major	C	1 octave on A string	♩ = 84	
Dominant 7th of Major Keys	C (starting on G), D (starting on A)	2 octaves	♩ = 104	
Diminished 7th of Minor Keys	A♭ (starting on G♮), B♭ (starting on A♮)	2 octaves	♩ = 104	
Double Stops				
Major in 6ths	G, B♭	1 octave	♩ = 72	

Ear Tests

Clapback

Candidates will choose to either clap or tap the rhythm of a short melody after the examiner has played it *twice* on the piano.

Time Signatures	Approximate Length
3/4 6/8	two to four measures

Example

1

2

Intervals

Candidates will be asked to identify the following intervals. The examiner will play each interval *once* in broken form on the piano.
or
Candidates may choose to sing or hum the following intervals. The examiner will play the first note *once* on the piano.

Above a Given Note	Below a Given Note
major and minor 3rds	major and minor 3rds
perfect 4th	
perfect 5th	perfect 5th
major and minor 6ths	
perfect octave	perfect octave

Playback

Candidates will be asked to play back a melody on the violin, based on the first five notes and the upper tonic of a major scale. The examiner will name the key, play the tonic triad *once,* and play the melody *twice* on the piano.

Beginning Note	Keys	Approximate Length
tonic, mediant, or dominant	C, G, D, A major	seven notes

Example only

Sight Reading

Playing

Candidates will be asked to play a short melody at sight. New features introduced at Grade 5 may include *pizzicato* and *arco* markings.

Difficulty	Time Signatures	Keys	Positions	Approximate Length
Grade 3 repertoire	2/4 3/4 4/4 3/8	C, F, G, D, A, E major	1st, 3rd	sixteen measures

Clapping

Candidates will be asked to clap or tap the rhythm of a melody. A steady pulse and rhythmic precision are expected.

Time Signatures	Approximate Length
3/4 4/4	four measures

Example only

Grade 6

Candidates in Grade 6 should have a well-developed brush stroke and be able to execute *collé* and *spiccato* strokes. Secure intonation in 1st to 5th positions is expected, including the ability to shift between positions with accuracy and fluency. Vibrato should be firmly established and used consistently where appropriate. A variety of dynamic levels should be evident.

Grade 6 Requirements	Marks
Repertoire	**60**
one selection from List A	17
one selection from List B	20
one selection from List C	17
Memory (3 marks each for List A and List C)	6
Technical Requirements	**20**
Etudes: *two* etudes from the *Syllabus* list	10
Technical Tests	10
– scales	
– arpeggios	
– double stops	
Ear Tests	**10**
Clapback	2
Intervals	3
Chords	2
Playback	3
Sight Reading	**10**
Playing	7
Clapping	3
Total possible marks (pass = 60)	**100**
Theory Co-requisite	
Intermediate Rudiments	

Repertoire

Please see "Examination Repertoire" on p. 9 for important information regarding this section of the examination.

Candidates must prepare *three* contrasting selections by three different composers: *one* from List A, *one* from List B, and *one* from List C.

Bullets used to denote selections for examination purposes:

- ● one selection
- ▶ selection is found in *Violin Series, 2013 Edition: Violin Repertoire* 6 FHM

List A

Concertos, *Airs variés*, and Fantasias

Dancla, Charles
Airs variés, op. 89 OTT; FIS; SCH
- ▶ Air varié on a Theme by Rossini (no. 2)
- ● Air varié on a Theme by Donizetti (no. 4)
- ● Air varié on a Theme by Mercadante (no. 6)

Huber, Adolph
Student Concertino in G Major, op. 6, no. 2 FIS
- ● 3rd movement

Komorowski, Anatoli
Concerto No. 2 in A Major PET
- ● 3rd movement: Allegro molto

Kymlicka, Milan
Concertino Grosso CAN
- ● 1st *and* 3rd movements

Mollenhauer, Eduard
- ▶ The Boy Paganini: Fantasia FIS (in *Solos for Young Violinists,* 2 ALF)

Portnoff, Leo
Concertino in A Minor, op. 14 BOS
- ● 1st movement

Rieding, Oskar
Concertino in A Minor (In Hungarian Style), op. 21 BAR; BOS
- ● 1st movement to *Andante sostenuto*

Concerto in G Major, op. 24 BOS
- ● 3rd movement

Seitz, Friedrich
Concerto No. 1 in D Major, op. 7 BOS; SCH
- ● 3rd movement

Concerto No. 2 in G Major, op. 13 BAR; BOS; SCH
- ● 1st movement

Concerto No. 5 in D Major, op. 22 BOS; SCH (in *Suzuki Violin School, Revised Edition,* 4 ALF; BAR)
- ● 3rd movement

Telemann, Georg Philipp
Concerto in G Major, op. 3, no. 3 PET
- ● 1st movement

Tessarini, Carlo
Concerto in G Major, op. 1, no. 3 (arr. Hermann Muller B&H)
- ● 1st movement

Vivaldi, Antonio
Concerto in G Major, op. 3, no. 3, RV 310 BAR; PET
- ▶ 1st movement (arr. Kathleen Wood FHM)

Concerto in A Minor, op. 3, no. 6, RV 356/F I:176 PET; (in *Suzuki Violin School, Revised Edition,* 4 ALF; BAR)
- ● 1st *or* 3rd movement

List B
Sonatas and Sonatinas

Handel, George Frideric
Sonata no. 3 in F Major, HWV 370 BAR; HEN; PET (in *Suzuki Violin School*, 6 ALF)
- ● *two* contrasting movements

Martinů, Bohuslav
Sonatina BAR
- ▶ 2nd *and* 3rd movements

Pepusch, Johann Christoph
6 Sonate da camera (transc. Walter Kolneder OTT)
Sonata No. 1 in B Minor
- ● *two* contrasting movements

Sonata No. 4 in D Minor
- ▶ 1st *and* 2nd movements
- ● 3rd *and* 4th movements

Sonata No. 6 in F Minor
- ● 1st *and* 4th movements

Telemann, Georg Philipp
Six Sonatas (1715) OTT
Sonata No. 1 in G Minor, TWV 41:g1
- ● *two* contrasting movements

Sonata No. 2 in D Major, TWV 41:D1
- ● *two* contrasting movements

Sonata No. 3 in B Minor, TWV 41:h1
- ● 3rd movement: Andante *and* 4th movement: Vivace

Sonata No. 4 in G Major, TWV 41:G1
- ● *two* contrasting movements

Sonata No. 6 in A Major, TWV 41:A1
- ● *two* contrasting movements

Veracini, Francesco
Twelve Sonatas, op. 1, 2 PET
Sonata No. 6 in A Minor
- ● 1st movement: Largo *and* 3rd movement: Allegro

Willan, Healey
Sonata No. 2 in E Major CMC
- ● Largo *and* Courante

List C
Concert Repertoire

Adaskin, Murray
- ▶ Daydreams CMC

Arnold, Malcolm
Four Scottish Dances, op. 59
- ● Scottish Dance No. 3 (arr. David Gedge, in *The Violin: A Collection* CHS)

Baxter, Timothy
- ● Jota (in *The Well-Tuned Fiddle*, Book II ABR)

Bennett, Richard Rodney
Six Country Dances
- ● Buskin (no. 2) (in *The Violin: A Collection* CHS)

Bohm, Carl
- ● Perpetuo mobile, from *Little Suite No. 6* FIS; (in *Solos for Young Violinists*, 3 ALF; in *Suzuki Violin School, Revised Edition*, 4 ALF)
- ● Sarabande in G Minor (in *Solos for Young Violinists*, 2 ALF)

Borowski, Felix
- ▶ Adoration PRE

Bridge, Frank
Three Pieces for Violin and Piano FAB
- ▶ Berceuse (no. 1)

Coulthard, Jean
- ● Rustic Dance, from *Little French Suite* (in *The Encore Series for Violin & Piano*, 6 FHM)

Coutts, George
- ▶ Hornpipe FHM

Cui, César
Kaleidoscope, op. 50 SIM
- ● Musette (no. 3)

Donkin, Christine
Fall Fair FHM
- ▶ Catch Me if You Can!

Donizetti, Gaetano
- ● Non giova il sospirar (arr. Charles-Auguste de Bériot, in *Romantic Violinist* B&H)

Drdla, František
- ● Tarantella, op. 27, no. 2 BOS

Ethridge, Jean
- ● Rondo brillante (in *The Encore Series for Violin & Piano*, 4 FHM)

Fauré, Gabriel
- ● Berceuse, op. 16 (in *The Violin Collection: Intermediate* SCH)

Fleming, Robert
- ● Something for Margot CMC

Gossec, François-Joseph
- ● Tambourin (arr. Sheila Nelson, in *Classical Violinist* B&H)

Grainger, Percy
- ● Molly on the Shore MAS

Kreisler, Fritz
- ▶ Andantino in the Style of Martini FIS
- ● Chanson Louis XIII et Pavane

Four Pieces for Violin and Piano FIS; MAS
- ● Aucassin und Nicolette

Massenet, Jules
- ▶ Invocation (Mélodie) from *Les Erinnyes*

Perlman, George
Israeli Concertino B&H
- ● Nocturne

Piazzolla, Astor
- ▶ Duo 1 (arr. Hywel Davies LIM)

Pishny-Floyd, Monte Keene
- ● Gavotte and Musette CMC

Rameau, Jean-Philippe
- ● Gavotte (in *Suzuki Violin School*, 6 ALF)

Reger, Max
- ● Romance BRH

Rieding, Oskar
- ● Petite Ballade BOS

Szelényi, István
Twenty-four Easy Little Concert Pieces
- ▶ Youngsters' Dance (no. 19) EMB; ABR

Technical Requirements

Please see "Technical Requirements" on p. 11 for important information regarding this section of the examination.

Etudes

Candidates must prepare *two* technically contrasting etudes from the following list.

Bullets used to denote selections for examination purposes:
- ● one selection
- ▶ selection is found in *Violin Series, 2013 Edition: Violin Technique and Etudes 5–8* FHM

Cohen, Mary
Technique Takes Off!, FAB
- ● Skater's Waltz (no. 11)

Dezaire, Nico
Violin Positions 4 & 5 DHM
- ● The Hunter
- ● Rock 'n' Roll

Kreutzer, Rodolphe
Quarante-deux études ou caprices INT
- ▶ Étude No. 4 in C Major
- ▶ Étude No. 2 in C Major
- ● *one* of nos. 3, 5, 6

Kayser, Heinrich Ernst
Elementary and Progressive Studies for the Violin, op. 20 SCH; FIS
- ● no. 14 *or* no. 17

Mazas, Jacques-Féréol
Études mélodiques et progressives, op. 36, book 1: *Études spéciales* SCH; INT
- ▶ Étude spéciale (no. 3: Fermeté d'archet)
- ● *one* of nos. 2, 5, 6, 10

Panofka, Heinrich
- ● no. 38 (in *Studies in Lyricism for Violin* FIS)

Trott, Josephine
Melodious Double Stops, 1 SCH
- ● *one* of nos. 17, 19–30

Melodious Double Stops, 2 SCH
- ▶ Melodious Double Stops No. 1
- ● no. 9 *or* no. 11

Wohlfahrt, Franz
Fifty Easy Melodic Studies, op. 74, 2 FIS
- ▶ Study in D Major (no. 44)
- ● no. 37 *or* no. 42

Sixty Studies for Violin, op. 45, 2 SCH
- ▶ Study in A Minor (no. 47)
- ● no. 43 *or* no. 50

Technical Tests

Please see "Technical Tests" on p. 11 for important information regarding this section of the examination.

Candidates must play all scales, arpeggios, and double stops from memory. Refer to *Violin Series, 2013 Edition: Violin Technique and Etudes 5–8* FHM for required patterns.

Scales	**Keys**	**Range**	**Tempo**	**Bowing**
Major	G, A	3 octaves	♩ = 100	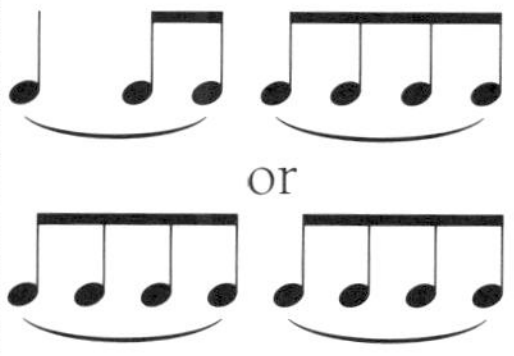
Harmonic and Melodic Minor	G, A			
Major	D♭	2 octaves	♩ = 100	
Harmonic and Melodic Minor	C♯			
Major	D	1 octave on A string	♩ = 88	
Harmonic and Melodic Minor	D			
Chromatic	on B♭, on B	2 octaves	♩ = 88	
Arpeggios				
Major	G, A	3 octaves	♩. = 54	
Minor	G, A			
Major	D♭	2 octaves	♩. = 54	
Minor	C♯			
Major	D	1 octave on A string	♩ = 88	
Minor	D			
Dominant 7th of Major Keys	F (starting on C), G (starting on D)	2 octaves	♩ = 88	
Diminished 7th of Minor Keys	C♯ (starting on B♯), E♭ (starting on D♮)	2 octaves	♩ = 88	
Double Stops				
Major in 3rds, 6ths, 8ves	G, A	1 octave	♩ = 76	
Harmonic Minor in 3rds, 6ths, 8ves	G, A			

Ear Tests

Clapback

Candidates will choose to either clap or tap the rhythm of a short melody after examiner has played it *twice* on the piano.

Time Signatures	Approximate Length
2/4 3/4 6/8	two to four measures

Example only

1

2

Intervals

Candidates will be asked to identify the following intervals. The examiner will play each interval *once* in broken form on the piano.

or

Candidates may choose to sing or hum the following intervals. The examiner will play the first note *once* on the piano.

Above a Given Note	Below a Given Note
major 2nd	
major and minor 3rds	major and minor 3rds
perfect 4th	perfect 4th
perfect 5th	perfect 5th
major and minor 6ths	minor 6th
perfect octave	perfect octave

Chords

Candidates will be asked to identify the following chords after the examiner has played the chord *once* in solid (blocked) form, close position on the piano.

Chords	Position
major and minor triads	root position

Playback

Candidates will be asked to play back a melody on the violin, based on a complete major scale (tonic to tonic, mediant to mediant, or dominant to dominant). The examiner will name the key, play the tonic triad *once*, and play the melody *twice* on the piano.

Beginning Note	Keys	Approximate Length
tonic, mediant, or dominant	C, G, D, A, E major	nine notes

Example only

Sight Reading

Playing

Candidates will be asked to play a short melody at sight. New features introduced at Grade 6 may include natural harmonics, left- and right-hand *pizzicato*, *appoggiaturas*, and double stops.

Difficulty	Time Signatures	Keys	Positions	Approximate Length
Grade 4 repertoire	$\frac{2}{4}$ $\frac{3}{4}$ $\frac{4}{4}$ $\frac{5}{4}$ $\frac{3}{8}$ $\frac{6}{8}$ ¢	C, F, G, D, A, E major A, E, D minor	1st, 2nd, 3rd	sixteen to twenty measures

Clapping

Candidates will be asked to clap or tap the rhythm of a melody. A steady pulse and rhythmic precision are expected.

Time Signatures	Approximate Length
$\frac{3}{4}$ $\frac{4}{4}$ $\frac{6}{8}$	four measures

Example only

Grade 7

Candidates in Grade 7 should have a well-developed *spiccato* stroke and be able to play with a wide dynamic range. Playing should show stylistic awareness. Fluency and accuracy up to 7th position is expected. Vibrato should pass from finger to finger and be used consistently to support repertoire where appropriate.

Grade 7 Requirements	Marks
Repertoire	**50**
one selection from List A	15 (1.5)
one selection from List B	20
one selection from List C	15 (1.5)
(The figures in parentheses for Lists A and C indicate the marks that will be deducted for selections that are not memorized.)	
Orchestral Excerpts	**10**
one excerpt from the *Syllabus* list	
Technical Requirements	**20**
Etudes: *one* etude from the *Syllabus* list	8
Technical Tests	12
– scales	
– arpeggios	
– double stops	
Ear Tests	**10**
Clapback	2
Intervals	3
Chords	2
Playback	3
Sight Reading	**10**
Playing	7
Clapping	3
Total possible marks (pass = 60)	**100**
Theory Co-requisite	
Advanced Rudiments	

Repertoire

Please see "Examination Repertoire" on p. 9 for important information regarding this section of the examination.

Candidates must prepare *three* contrasting selections by three different composers: *one* from List A, *one* from List B, and *one* from List C.

Bullets used to denote selections for examination purposes:

- ● one selection
- ▶ selection is found in *Violin Series, 2013 Edition: Violin Repertoire 7* FHM

List A
Concertos, *Airs variés*, and Fantasias

Corelli, Arcangelo
- ● La Folia (arr. Shin'ichi Suzuki, in *Suzuki Violin School,* 6 ALF)

Dancla, Charles
Airs variés, op. 89 OTT; FIS; SCH
- ● Air varié on a Theme by Bellini (no. 3)
- ● Air varié on a Theme by Weigl (no. 5) (in *Solos for Young Violinists,* 3 ALF)

Farmer, Henry
- ▶ Hope Told a Flattering Tale (in *Romantic Violinist* B&H)

Marcello, Benedetto
Concerto in D Major OTT
- ● 1st movement

Nardini, Pietro
Concerto in E Minor AUG; INT
- ● 1st movement

Perlman, George
Israeli Concertino B&H
- ● 3rd movement: Fantasie-Recitative

Rieding, Oskar
Concerto in G Major, op. 24 BOS
- ● 1st movement (in *Solos for Young Violinists,* 2 ALF)

Seitz, Friedrich
Concerto No. 1 in D Major, op. 7 BOS; SCH
- ● 1st movement

Concerto No. 3 in G Minor, op. 12 BAR; BOS; SCH
- ▶ 1st movement (abridged) (in *Solos for Young Violinists,* 2 ALF)

Stamitz, Anton
Concerto in G Major OTT
- ● 1st movement

Vivaldi, Antonio
Concerto in G Minor, op. 12, no. 1, RV 317/F I:221 OTT; INT (in *Suzuki Violin School, Revised Edition,* 5 ALF)
- ● 1st movement

List B
Sonatas and Sonatinas

Anonymous
Sonata in D Minor (arr. Hugh J. McLean, in *Musica da Camera,* no. 103 OUP)
- ● 1st movement: Preludio *and* 7th movement: Giga
- ▶ 2nd movement: Fugato *and* 3rd movement: Allemanda (arr. Kathleen Wood)

Bach, Johann Christian
Sonata in D Major, op. 16, no. 1 ZIM
- ▶ 1st movement: Allegro assai *and* 2nd movement: Andante grazioso

Benda, František
Sonata in A Minor
- ● Tempo di Minuetto (in *Classical Violinist* B&H)

Corelli, Arcangelo
12 Sonate, op. 5 BAR; OTT
Sonata No. 1 in D Major
- ● 4th movement: Adagio *and* 5th movement: Allegro

Sonata No. 3 in C Major
- ● 1st movement: Adagio *and* 2nd movement: Allegro

Sonata No. 4 in F Major
- ● 1st movement: Adagio *and* 2nd movement: Allegro

Sonata No. 5 in G Minor
- ● 3rd movement: Adagio *and* 4th movement: Vivace

Eccles, Henry
Sonata in G Minor INT (in *Suzuki Violin School,* 8 ALF)
- ● *two* contrasting movements

Handel, George Frideric
Sonata No. 2 in G Minor, HWV 368 BAR; HEN; PET
- ● 1st *and* 2nd movements
- ● 1st *and* 4th movements

Sonata No. 4 in D Major, HWV 371 BAR; HEN; PET (in *Suzuki Violin School,* 6 ALF)
- ● *two* contrasting movements

Sonata No. 6 in E Major, HWV 373 BAR; HEN; PET
- ● *two* contrasting movements

Mendelssohn, Felix
Sonata in F Major (1820) BAR
- ▶ 1st movement: Allegro

Mozart, Wolfgang Amadeus
Sonata in E Minor, K 304 BAR; HEN
- ● 1st movement

Schubert, Franz
Sonatina in D Major, op. posth. 137, no. 1, D 384 BAR; HEN
- ● *two* contrasting movements

Vivaldi, Antonio
Sonata in F Major, op. 2, no. 4, RV 20/F XIII:32
- ● 1st *and* 2nd movements

Weber, Carl Maria von
Six sonates progressives pour le pianoforte avec violin obligé, op. 10b HEN
Sonata No. 1 in F Major
- ● *two* contrasting movements

Sonata No. 3 in D Major
- ● 1st *and* 2nd movements

Sonata No. 6 in C Major
- ● 1st *and* 3rd movements

List C
Concert Repertoire

Barnes, Milton
Three Folk Dances CMC
- ● Folk Dance No. 3

Bartók, Béla
- ● Evening in the Country, from *Ten Easy Pieces* (transc. Tibor Fülep EMB)

Bohm, Carl
Arabesken
- ▶ Introduction and Polonaise (no. 12) FIS (in *Solos for Young Violinists,* 2 ALF)

Bridge, Frank
Three Pieces for Violin and Piano FAB
- ▶ Cradle Song (no. 3)
- ● Serenade (no. 2)

Copland, Aaron
Old American Songs, 2
- ● Ching-a-Ring Chaw (Minstrel Song) (in *Copland for Violin* B&H)
- ● The Little Horses (Lullaby) (in *Copland for Violin* B&H)

Cui, César
Kaleidoscope, op. 50 SIM
- ● Perpetuum mobile (no. 12)
- ▶ Scherzetto (no. 22)

Elgar, Edward
- ● Chanson du matin NOV
- ▶ Chanson de nuit NOV

Fiocco, Joseph Hector
- ● Allegro (in G Major) BAR; INT; OTT (in *Suzuki Violin School,* 6 ALF)

Fleming, Robert
- ● Recollections CMC

Gluck, Christoph Willibald
- ● Mélodie *(Dance of the Blessed Spirits),* from *Orfeo ed Euridice* (arr. Fritz Kreisler OTT and in *Solos for Young Violinists,* 4 ALF)

Gratton, Hector
- ● Première Danse Canadienne CMC

Heuberger, Richard
- ● Midnight Bells, from *Der Opernball,* op. 40 (arr. Fritz Kreisler, in *The Fritz Kreisler Collection,* 2 FIS; *Music from the Romantic Era* BOS)

Järnefelt, Armas
- ▶ Berceuse CHS

Kreisler, Fritz
- ● Liebesleid FIS
- ● Menuet in the Style of Porpora OTT
- ● Rondino on a Theme by Beethoven FIS (in *Solos for Young Violinists,* 4 ALF)
- ▶ Syncopation OTT (in *The Fritz Kreisler Collection,* 2 FIS)
- ● Tempo di Minuetto in the Style of Pugnani OTT (in *Solos for Young Violinists,* 3 ALF)

Mascagni, Pietro
- ● Intermezzo sinfonico, from *Cavalleria rusticana* (arr. FIS; SCH)

Młynarski, Emil
- ● Mazurka (arr. Barbara Barber, in *Solos for Young Violinists,* 3 ALF)

Mondonville, Jean-Joseph Cassanéa de
Sonata No. 3 in G Major (in *Solos for the Violin Player* SCH)
- ● 4th movement: Tambourin

Moszkowski, Moritz
Spanische Tänze, op. 12, PET
- ▶ Spanischer Tänz No. 1

Paradis, Maria Theresia von
- ● Sicilienne OTT (in *Solos for Young Violinists,* 6 ALF)

Piazzolla, Astor
- ▶ Ausencias (arr. Hywel Davies LIM)

Polson, Arthur
- ● A Dream CMC

Potstock, William H.
- ● Souvenir de Sarasate FIS (in *Solos for Young Violinists,* 3 ALF)

Raff, Joachim
Six Morceaux, op. 85
- ● Cavatina (no. 3) EMB

Ravel, Maurice
- ● Pavane pour une infante défunte OTT

Severn, Edmund
- ● Polish Dance FIS (in *Solos for Young Violinists,* 4 ALF)

Sheng, Bright
Three Fantasies for Violin and Piano SCH
- ● Dream Song (no. 1)

Shostakovich, Dmitri
- ● Spring Waltz, op. 27, no. 6 (arr. Konstantin Fortunatov in *Shostakovich: Albumstücke* PET)

Toselli, Enrico
- ● Serenade, op. 6 (arr. Fredric Fradkin BMC)

Valdez, Charles Robert
- ● Sérénade du tzigane (Gypsy Serenade) (arr. Fritz Kreisler in *Favourite Encore Folio* FIS)

Vaughan Williams, Ralph
- ● Fantasia on Greensleeves, from *Sir John in Love* (arr. Michael Mullinar OUP)

Veracini, Francesco Maria
Sonata in D Minor
- ● Gigue (in *Suzuki Violin School, Revised Edition,* 5 ALF)

Wachs, Paul
- ▶ Air de Ballet (in *The Violinist's Contest Album* FIS)

Weber, Carl Maria von
- ● Country Dance (in *Suzuki Violin School, Revised Edition,* 5 ALF)

Wieniawski, Henryk
- ● Kujawiak (Mazurka) (COM)

Orchestral Excerpts

Candidates should be prepared to play the first violin part of *one* excerpt from the following list. Candidates are encouraged to listen to and become familiar with the works from which these excerpts are taken. The candidate's ability to perform excerpts in a manner that demonstrates an understanding of the style and context is an important examination criterion. For instructions regarding the performance of chords, please see p. 11.

- All orchestral excerpts are included in *Violin Series, 2013 Edition: Orchestral Excerpts* FHM.
- Alternatively, candidates may use standard published orchestral parts for the specific excerpts. The list below includes measure numbers for reference.

Each bulleted item (▶) represents one selection for examination purposes.

Beethoven, Ludwig van
Symphony No. 5 in C Minor, op. 67
- ▶ 2nd movement: mm. 15–48, 77–86, 106–114

Bizet, George
Carmen Suite No. 1
- ▶ Les Toréadors (no. 5): mm. 1–101 (first eighth note)

Elgar, Edward
Serenade for String Orchestra, op. 20
- ▶ 1st movement: mm. 92–137 *and* 2nd movement: mm. 1–32

Handel, George Frideric
Messiah, HWV 56
- ▶ Overture ("Symphony"): complete (mm. 1–97)

Haydn, Franz Joseph
String Quartet in C Major ("The Bird"), Hob. III:39
- ▶ 1st movement: mm. 1–59

Symphony No. 49 in F Minor ("La passione"), Hob. I:49
- ▶ 2nd movement: mm. 1–51

Mendelssohn, Felix
String Quartet in E flat Major, op. 12
- ▶ 2nd movement (Canzonetta): mm. 1–49

Mozart, Wolfgang Amadeus
Symphony No. 29 in A Major, K 201
- ▶ 1st movement: mm. 1–77 (beat 2)

Technical Requirements

Please see "Technical Requirements" on p. 11 for important information regarding this section of the examination.

Etudes

Candidates must prepare *one* etude from the following list.

Bullets used to denote selections for examination purposes:
- ● one selection
- ▶ selection is found in *Violin Series, 2013 Edition: Violin Technique and Etudes 5–8* FHM

Barlowe, Amy
Twelve Etude-Caprices in the Styles of the Great Composers ALF
- ▶ In the Style of Beethoven (no. 6)

Cohen, Mary
Technique Flies High! FAB
- ▶ Wild Fire

Dont, Jacob
Twenty-four Exercises, op. 37 INT; SCH
- ● *one* of nos. 1–7

Kayser, Heinrich Ernst
Elementary and Progressive Studies for the Violin, op. 20 SCH; FIS
- ● no. 33

Kreutzer, Rodolphe
Quarante-deux études ou caprices INT
- ▶ Étude No. 11 in E Major
- ● *one* of nos. 7–9, 13

Mazas, Jacques-Féréol
Études mélodiques et progressives, op. 36, book 1: *Études spéciales* SCH; INT
- ▶ Division of the Bow in the *Cantilena* (no. 8)
- ▶ The Mordant (no. 15)
- ● *one* of nos. 9, 17, 21, 28

Polo, Enrico
30 Studi a Corde Doppie RIC
- ● no. 10

Trott, Josephine
Melodious Double Stops, 2 SCH
- ▶ Melodious Double Stops (no. 17)
- ● no. 14 *or* no. 16

Technical Tests

Please see "Technical Tests" on p. 11 for important information regarding this section of the examination.

Candidates must play all scales, arpeggios, and double stops from memory. Refer to *Violin Series, 2013 Edition: Violin Technique and Etudes 5–8* FHM for required patterns.

Scales	Keys	Range	Tempo	Bowing
Major	A♭, B♭, C	3 octaves	♩ = 120	
Harmonic and Melodic Minor	G♯, B♭, C			
Major Artificial Harmonics	G	1 octave	♩ = 80	
Chromatic	on C, on D	2 octaves	♩ = 108	
Arpeggios				
Major	A♭, B♭, C	3 octaves	♩. = 72	
Minor	G♯, B♭, C			
Dominant 7th of Major Keys	D (starting on A), E♭ (starting on B♭)	3 octaves	♩ = 100	
Diminished 7th of Minor Keys	B♭ (starting on A♮), B (starting on A♯)	3 octaves	♩ = 100	
Double Stops				
Major in 3rds, 6ths, and 8ves	B♭, C	1 octave	♩ = 92	
Harmonic Minor in 3rds, 6ths, and 8ves	B♭, C			

Ear Tests

Clapback

Candidates will choose to either clap or tap the rhythm of a short melody after the examiner has played it *twice* on the piano.

Time Signatures	Approximate Length
2/4 3/4 6/8	four measures

Example only

1

2

Intervals

Candidates will be asked to identify the following intervals. The examiner will play each interval *once* in broken form on the piano.
or
Candidates may choose to sing or hum the following intervals. The examiner will play the first note *once* on the piano.

Above a Given Note	Below a Given Note
major and minor 2nds	
major and minor 3rds	major and minor 3rds
perfect 4th	perfect 4th
perfect 5th	perfect 5th
major and minor 6ths	minor 6th
	major 7th
perfect octave	perfect octave

Chords

Candidates will be asked to identify the following chords after the examiner has played the chord *once* in solid (blocked) form, close position on the piano.

Chords	Position
major and minor triads	root position
dominant 7th	root position

Playback

Candidates will be asked to play back a melody on the violin, based on a complete major scale (tonic to tonic, mediant to mediant, or dominant to dominant). The examiner will name the key, play the tonic triad *once*, and play the melody *twice* on the piano.

Beginning Note	Keys	Approximate Length
tonic, mediant, dominant, or upper tonic	C, G, D, A, E major	nine notes

Example only

Sight Reading

Playing

Candidates will be asked to play a short melody at sight. New features introduced at Grade 7 may include trills, grace notes, triple stops, and *spiccato*.

Difficulty	Time Signatures	Keys	Positions	Approximate Length
Grade 5 repertoire	$\frac{2}{4}$ $\frac{3}{4}$ $\frac{4}{4}$ $\frac{5}{4}$ $\frac{3}{8}$ $\frac{6}{8}$ ¢	C, F, B♭, G, D, A major A, D, E, B minor	1st to 4th	sixteen to twenty measures

Clapping

Candidates will be asked to clap or tap the rhythm of a melody. A steady pulse and rhythmic precision are expected.

Time Signatures	Approximate Length
$\frac{2}{4}$ $\frac{3}{4}$ $\frac{4}{4}$ $\frac{6}{8}$	four measures

Example only

Grade 8

Candidates in Grade 8 should have well developed *spiccato*, *sautillé*, and *ricochet* strokes. Playing should show stylistic awareness. Fluency and accuracy up to 7th position are expected. Vibrato should pass from finger to finger and be used consistently to support repertoire where appropriate.

Grade 8 Requirements	Marks
Repertoire *one* selection from List A *one* selection from List B *one* selection from List C *one* selection from List D (The figures in parentheses for Lists A, C, and D indicate the marks that will be deducted for selections that are not memorized.)	**50** 15 (1.5) 15 10 (1) 10 (1)
Orchestral Excerpts *two* contrasting excerpts from the *Syllabus* list	**10**
Technical Requirements Etudes: *one* etude from the *Syllabus* list Technical Tests – scales – arpeggios – double stops	**20** 8 12
Ear Tests Intervals Chords Cadences Playback	**10** 3 2 2 3
Sight Reading Playing Clapping	**10** 7 3
Total possible marks (pass = 60)	**100**
Theory Co-requisites Advanced Rudiments Introductory Harmony (recommended)	

Repertoire

Candidates must prepare *four* contrasting selections: *one* from List A, *one* from List B, *one* from List C, and *one* from List D. Candidates are encouraged to select repertoire in a variety of keys and tempos, with no more than two works from the same era (for example, only two selections from the Baroque era).

Bullets used to denote selections for examination purposes:

- ● one selection
- ▶ selection is found in *Violin Series, 2013 Edition: Violin Repertoire 8* FHM

Please note that *cadenzas* are required where indicated. Unless otherwise noted, any *cadenza* is acceptable, as long as the examiner is provided with an original copy of the music, and it is equivalent in difficulty to the standard *cadenza* for that work.

List A
Concertos, *Airs variés*, and Fantasias

Accolay, Jean-Baptiste
- ● Concerto in A Minor, op. 12 BAR; FIS; INT (in *Solos for Young Violinists*, 3 ALF)

Bach, Johann Sebastian
Concerto in A Minor, BWV 1041 BAR; INT (in *Suzuki Violin School*, 7 ALF)
- ● 1st movement

Benda, Johann
Concerto in G major (arr. Samuel Dushkin OTT)
- ● 1st movement

Dancla, Charles
Airs variés, op. 118 FIS
- ● I Montecchi e I Capuletti (no. 1)
- ● Norma (no. 3)
- ● La Somnambula (no. 4)
- ▶ La Straniera (no. 2)

Bériot, Charles-Auguste de
Concerto in B Minor, op. 32 PET
- ● 1st movement
- ● 3rd movement: Rondo Russe

Haydn, Franz Joseph
Concerto in G Major, Hob. VIIa:4 (ed. Ferdinand Küchler HEN)
- ▶ 1st movement (with *cadenza* by Franz Beyer)
  → begin at m. 20

Komarowski, Anatoli
Concerto No. 1 in E Minor PET
- ▶ 1st movement (with *cadenza*)

Seitz, Friedrich
Concerto No. 4 in D Major, op. 15 BOS; SCH
- ● 1st movement

List B
Sonatas and Sonatinas

Adaskin, Murray
Sonata No. 1 (for solo violin) CMC
- ● 1st movement: Andante)
- ● 2nd movement: Adagio

Albinoni, Tomaso
Sonata in D Major, op. 6, no. 7 EMA
- ● *two* contrasting movements

Sonata in G Minor, op. 6, no. 2 OTT; EMA
- ● 1st *and* 2nd movements

Bartók, Béla
Sonatina (transc. André Gertler EMB)
- ● 1st movement: Bagpipers *and* 2nd movement: Bear Dance

Corelli, Arcangelo
12 Sonate, op. 5 BAR; OTT
Sonata No. 6 in A Major
- ● 1st movement: Grave *and* 5th movement: Allegro

Dvořák, Antonín
Sonatina in G Major, op. 100 BAR; FIS
- ● 1st movement: Allegro risoluto *and* 2nd movement: Larghetto
- ▶ 2nd movement: Larghetto *and* 3rd movement: Molto vivace

Elsner, Józef
Sonata in F Major, op. 10, no. 1 PWM
- ▶ 1st movement: Allegro

Handel, George Frideric
Sonata No. 1 in A Major, HWV 361 BAR; HEN; PET (in *Suzuki Violin School*, 7 ALF)
- ● 1st *and* 2nd movements
- ● 1st *and* 4th movements

Sonata No. 5 in A Major, HWV 372 BAR; HEN; PET
- ● 1st *and* 2nd movements
- ● 1st *and* 4th movements

Mozart, Wolfgang Amadeus
Sonata in G Major, K 293a (301) BAR; HEN
- ● 1st *or* 2nd movement

Schubert, Franz
Sonatina in G Minor, op. posth. 137, no. 3, D 408 BAR; HEN
- ● 1st *and* 2nd movements

Tartini, Giuseppe
12 Sonate e una pastorale, op. 1
Sonata No. 1 in A Major, BA14 MAS
- ● 1st movement: Grave *and* 3rd movement: Presto

Sonata No. 4 in G Major, BG17 PET; KAL
- ● 1st movement: Grave *and* 2nd movement: Fuga

12 Sonate, op. 2 ZAN
Sonata No. 1 in D Major, BD13
- ● 3rd movement: Affettuoso *and* 4th movement: Allegro assai

Sonata No. 2 in G Major, BG18
- ● 1st movement: Andante affettuoso *and* 3rd movement: Allegro

Sonata No. 6 in C Major, BC12
- ● 1st movement: Largo andante *and* 3rd movement: Presto assai

Vivaldi, Antonio
Sonata op. 2, no. 7 (Realizzazione di Federico Mompellio) ZAN
- ● 1st movement: Preludio *and* 2nd movement: Allemanda

List C
Concert Repertoire

Boulanger, Lili
Deux Morceaux SCH (in *Violinmusik von Komponistinnen* OTT)
- ● Cortège (no. 2)
- ● Nocturne (no. 1)

Champagne, Claude
- ● Danse villageoise BER; CMC

d'Ambrosio, Alfredo
- ● Canzonetta (in *Romantic Violinist* B&H)

Daquin, Lous-Claude
- ● Le coucou from *Premier livre de pièces de clavecin* (arr. Györgyi Répássy EMB)

Debussy, Claude
- ● La fille aux cheveux de lin (transc. Arthur Hartmann DUR)

Elgar, Edward
- ● Salut D'Amour OTT

Glazunov, Aleksandr
- ▶ Albumblatt (transc. Jean-François Gonzales MPB)

Have, Willem ten
- ▶ Allegro brillant, op. 19 FIS

Healey, Derek E.
Six Epigrams CMC
- ● nos. 2, 5, *and* 6

Korngold, Erich Wolfgang
- ● Gartenszene from *Viel Lärmen um nichts*, op. 11 (in *Vier Stücke* OTT)

Kreisler, Fritz
- ● La gitana FIS
- ● Liebesfreud FIS
- ▶ Schön Rosmarin FIS
- ● Sicilienne and Rigaudon in the Style of Francoeur FIS; OTT (in *Solos for Young Violinists*, 5 ALF)

Kulesha, Gary
Song and Dance
- ▶ Dance CMC

Levkovich, Alexander
- ● Lullaby CMC

Martinů, Bohuslav
Intermezzo BAR
- ● Andante (no. 3)
- ● Poco allegro (no. 4)

Massenet, Jules
- ● Méditation, from *Thaïs* PET (transc. M.P. Marsick UMP; in *Solos for Young Violinists*, 5 ALF)

Monti, Vittorio
- ● Csárdás RIC; FIS; (in *Solos for Young Violinists*, 5 ALF; BAR)

Morley, Angela
- ● Rêverie for Violin and Piano NOV

Morlock, Jocelyn
- ● Dervish CMC

Moszkowski, Moritz
Spanische Tänze, op. 12 PET
- ● Spanischer Tänz (no. 2)

Perrault, Michel Brunet
- ▶ Solitude BER

Ries, Franz Anton
- ● Perpetuum mobile, op. 34, no. 5 FIS

Sarasate, Pablo de
- ● Playera (Spanish Dance, op. 23, no. 5) (in *Romantic Violinist* B&H)

Schubert, François
Bagatelles, op. 13
- ▶ Die Biene (no. 9) EMB

Schumann, Robert
- ● Vogel als Prophet, from *Waldscenen,* op. 82, no. 7 (transc. Leopold Auer ZIM)

Drei Romanzen, op. 94 PET
- ● Romance No. 2 (arr. Fritz Kreisler OTT)
- ● Romance No. 3

Senaillé, Jean-Baptiste
- ● Les polichinelles (arr. Alfred Moffat OTT)

Shostakovich, Dmitri
- ▶ Romance, from *Ovod (The Gadfly),* op. 97 (arr. Konstantin Fortunatov, in *Shostakovich: Albumstücke* PET)

Sibelius, Jean
Five Pieces, op. 81
- ● Rondino (no. 2) B&H

Smetana, Bedřich
From the Homeland (Z domoviny) BAR
- ▶ 1st movement: Moderato

Wieniawski, Henryk
Two Mazurkas, op. 19 PWM; MAS; PET
- ▶ Mazurka (Obertass) (no. 1)
- ● Mazurka (Le ménétrier) (no. 2) EMB

Willeke, Willem
- ● Chant sans paroles (arr. Fritz Kreisler in *Favorite Encore Folio* FIS)

List D
Unaccompanied Repertoire

Bach, Johann Sebastian
Partita No. 2 in D Minor, BWV 1004 BAR; HEN
- ▶ 4th movement: Giga

Partita No. 3 in E Major, BWV 1006 BAR; HEN
- ▶ 6th movement: Bourrée
- ● 7th movement: Gigue

Telemann, Georg Philipp
Twelve Fantasias for Violin BAR; INT
Fantasia No. 1 in B flat Major, TWV 40:14
- ● 1st movement: Largo

Fantasia No. 7 in E flat Major, TWV 40:20
- ▶ 1st movement: Dolce
- ● 2nd movement: Allegro

Fantasia No. 8 in E Major, TWV 40:21
- ● 2nd movement: Spirituoso

Fantasia No. 12 in A Minor, TWV 40:25
- ● 1st movement: Moderato
- ● 2nd movement: Vivace

Orchestral Excerpts

Candidates should be prepared to play the first violin part of *two* contrasting excerpts by two different composers from the following list. Candidates are encouraged to listen to and become familiar with the works from which these excerpts are taken. The candidate's ability to perform excerpts in a manner that demonstrates an understanding of the style and context is an important examination criterion. For instructions regarding the performance of chords please see p. 11.

- All orchestral excerpts are included in *Violin Series, 2013 Edition: Orchestral Excerpts* FHM.
- Alternatively, candidates may use standard published orchestral parts for the specific excerpts. The list below includes measure numbers for reference.

Each bulleted item (▶) represents one selection for examination purposes.

Bach, Johann Sebastian
Brandenburg Concerto No. 3 in G Major, BWV 1048
- ▶ 3rd movement: mm. 1–18 (second eighth note), mm. 24–35 (beat 1)

Beethoven, Ludwig van
Symphony No. 2 in D Major, op. 36
- ▶ 3rd movement: mm. 1–84 *and* 4th movement: mm. 1–25

Grieg, Edvard
Holberg Suite, op. 40
- ▶ 1st movement (Prelude): mm. 1–30 *and* 4th movement (Air): mm. 1–29

Haydn, Franz Joseph
Symphony No. 94 in G Major ("Surprise"), Hob. I:94
- ▶ 2nd movement: mm. 1–24, 49–74, 107–114

Mozart, Wolfgang Amadeus
String Quartet in D Minor, K 421
- ▶ 1st movement: mm. 1–41 *and* 3rd movement: Menuetto and Trio (complete)

Symphony No. 25 in G Minor, K 183
- ▶ 1st movement: mm. 1–12, 29–83 (beat 1)

Saint-Saëns, Camille
Le carnaval des animaux
- ▶ 14th movement (*Final*): mm. 53–92

Technical Requirements

Please see "Technical Requirements" on p. 11 for important information regarding this section of the examination.

Etudes

Candidates must prepare *one* etude from the following list.

Bullets used to denote selections for examination purposes:
- ● one selection
- ▶ selection is found in *Violin Series, 2013 Edition: Violin Technique and Etudes 5–8* FHM

Barlowe, Amy
Twelve Etude-Caprices in the Styles of the Great Composers ALF
- ▶ In the Style of Bach (no. 2)

Campagnoli, Bartolomeo
7 Divertimenti, op. 18 RIC; KMA
Divertimento No. 2
- ▶ Polonaise and Trio
  - → play in 2nd position

Dont, Jacob
Twenty-four Exercises, op. 37 INT; SCH
- ● *one* of nos. 8–12

Fiorillo, Federigo
Étude de violon formant 36 caprices, op. 3 INT; SCH
- ▶ Caprice in B flat Major (no. 5)
- ▶ Caprice in E flat Major (no. 6)
- ● *one* of nos. 3, 16, 28

Kreutzer, Rodolphe
Quarante-deux études ou caprices INT
- ▶ Étude No. 12 in A Minor
- ● *one* of nos. 10, 14–17

Mazas, Jacques-Féréol
Études mélodiques et progressives, op. 36, book 1: *Études spéciales* SCH; INT
- ▶ Étude spéciale (no. 30: Ronde Villageoise)

Études mélodiques et progressives, op. 36, book 2: *Études brillantes* SCH; INT
- ▶ Étude brillante (no. 34: Staccato)
- ● *one* of nos. 33, 35, 39

Polo, Enrico
30 Studi a Corde Doppie RIC
- ● no. 15 *or* no. 23

Technical Tests

Please see "Technical Tests" on p. 11 for important information regarding this section of the examination.

Candidates must play all scales, arpeggios, and double stops from memory. Refer to *Violin Series, 2013 Edition: Violin Technique and Etudes 5–8* FHM for required patterns.

Scales	Keys	Range	Tempo	Bowing
Major	B, D♭, D	3 octaves	♩ = 138	
Harmonic and Melodic Minor	B, C♯, D			
Major Artificial Harmonics	A, B♭	1 octave	♩ = 108	
Chromatic	on G, on A, on B♭	3 octaves	♩ = 120	
Arpeggios				
Major	B, D♭, D	3 octaves	♩. = 84	
Minor	B, C♯, D			
Dominant 7th of Major Keys	D♭ (starting on A♭), E (starting on B), F (starting on C)	3 octaves	♩ = 108	
Diminished 7th of Minor Keys	A (starting on G♯), C (starting on B♮), C♯ (starting on B♯)	3 octaves	♩ = 108	
Double Stops				
Major in 3rds, 6ths, 8ves	G, A	2 octaves	♩ = 72	
Harmonic Minor in 3rds, 6ths, 8ves	G, A			
Melodic Minor in 3rds, 6ths, 8ves	G, A	1 octave	♩ = 72	

Ear Tests

Intervals

Candidates will be asked to identify the following intervals. The examiner will play each interval *once* in broken form on the piano.

or

Candidates may choose to sing or hum the following intervals. The examiner will play the first note *once* on the piano.

Above a Given Note	Below a Given Note
major and minor 2nds	major 2nd
major and minor 3rds	major and minor 3rds
perfect 4th	perfect 4th
perfect 5th	perfect 5th
major and minor 6ths	minor 6th
minor 7th	major 7th
perfect octave	perfect octave

Chords

Candidates will be asked to identify the following chords after the examiner has played the chord *once* in solid (blocked) form, close position on the piano.

Chords	Position
major and minor triads	root position
dominant 7th	root position
diminished 7th	root position

Cadences

Candidates will be asked to identify the following cadences by name or symbols. The examiner will play the tonic chord *once*, and then *twice* play a short phrase ending in a cadence.

Name of Cadence	Symbols
perfect or authentic	V–I
plagal	IV–I

Example only

Perfect (Authentic)

Playback

Candidates will be asked to play back a melody on the violin, approximately one octave in range. The examiner will name the key, play the tonic triad *once*, and play the melody *twice* on the piano.

Beginning Note	Keys	Approximate Length
tonic, mediant, dominant, or upper tonic	C, G, D, A, E major	nine notes

Example only

Sight Reading

Playing

Candidates will be asked to play a short melody at sight. New features introduced at Grade 8 may include chromatic passages, mordants, and artificial harmonics.

Difficulty	Time Signatures	Keys	Positions	Approximate Length
Grade 6 repertoire	2/4 3/4 4/4 5/4 3/8 6/8 ¢	C, F, B♭, G, D, A, E major A, D, G, E, B, C♯ minor	1st to 5th	sixteen to twenty measures

Clapping

Candidates will be asked to clap or tap the rhythm of a melody. A steady pulse and rhythmic precision are expected.

Time Signatures	Approximate Length
2/4 3/4 4/4 6/8	four measures

Example only

Grade 9

Candidates in Grade 9 should be able to execute all bow strokes and maintain control and security in any position. A mature, singing tone with an expressive and varied vibrato is expected. Playing should exhibit stylistic awareness.

Grade 9 Requirements	Marks
Repertoire *one* selection from List A *one* selection from List B *one* selection from List C *one* selection from List D (The figures in parentheses for Lists A, C, and D indicate the marks that will be deducted for selections that are not memorized.)	**50** 15 (1.5) 15 10 (1) 10 (1)
Orchestral Excerpts *two* contrasting excerpts from the *Syllabus* list	**10**
Technical Requirements Etudes: *one* etude from the *Syllabus* list Technical Tests – scales – arpeggios – double stops	**20** 8 12
Ear Tests Intervals Chords Cadences Playback	**10** 3 2 2 3
Sight Reading Playing Clapping	**10** 7 3
Total possible marks (pass = 60)	**100**
Theory Co-requisites Advanced Rudiments Basic Harmony *or* Basic Keyboard Harmony History 1: An Overview	

Repertoire

Please see "Examination Repertoire" on p. 9 for important information regarding this section of the examination.

Candidates must prepare *four* contrasting selections: *one* from List A, *one* from List B, *one* from List C, and *one* from List D. Candidates are encouraged to select repertoire in a variety of keys and tempos, with no more than two works from the same era (for example, only two selections from the Baroque era).

Each bulleted item (●) represents one selection for examination purposes.

Please note that *cadenzas* are required where indicated. Unless otherwise indicated, any *cadenza* is acceptable, as long as the examiner is provided with an original copy of the music, and it is equivalent in difficulty to the standard *cadenza* for that work.

List A

Concertos

Bériot, Charles-Auguste de
Concerto No. 1 in D Major, op. 16 PET
- 1st movement (to first *tutti*)

Concerto No. 7 in G Major, op. 76 FIS
- 1st movement

Concerto No. 9 in A Minor, op. 104 PET
- 1st *and* 2nd movements
- 2nd *and* 3rd movements

Haydn, Franz Joseph
Concerto No. 1 in C Major Hob. VIIa:1 HEN; PET
- 1st movement (with *cadenza*) *and* 2nd movement (with *cadenza*)

Kreutzer, Rodolphe
Concerto No. 13 in D Major FIS
- 1st *and* 2nd movements

Mozart, Wolfgang Amadeus
Concerto in B flat Major, K 207 BAR; PET; INT
- 1st movement (with *cadenza*) *and* 2nd movement (with *cadenza*)

Concerto in D Major, K 211 BAR; PET; INT
- 1st movement (with *cadenza*) *and* 2nd movement (with *cadenza*)

Concerto in G Major, K 216 BAR; PET; INT
- 1st movement (with *cadenza*) *and* 2nd movement (with *cadenza*)

Rieding, Oskar
Concerto in D Major, op. 5 BUT
- complete

Concerto in E Minor, op. 7 BOS
- complete

Rode, Pierre
- Air varié (in *Classical Violinist* B&H)

Concerto No. 7 in A Minor, op. 9 SCH; INT
- 1st movement (with *cadenza*) *and* 2nd movement
- 2nd *and* 3rd movement

Concerto No. 8 in E Minor, op. 13 SCH; PET
- 1st *and* 2nd movements

Viotti, Giovanni Battista
Concerto No. 23 in G Major PET
- 1st movement (with *cadenza*) *and* 2nd movement (with *cadenza*)

Vivaldi, Antonio
Il cimento dell'armonia e dell'inventione, op. 8 BAR
- Concerto No. 1 in E Major (La primavera), RV 269
- Concerto No. 2 in G Minor (L'estate), RV 315
- Concerto No. 3 in F Major (L'autunno), RV 293
- Concerto No. 4 in F Minor (L'inverno), RV 297

List B
Sonatas and Sonatinas

Adaskin, Murray
Sonatine baroque for solo violin RIC; CMC
- 3rd movement

Beethoven, Ludwig van
Sonata in D Major, op. 12, no. 1 HEN
- 1st movement

Sonata in A Major, op. 12, no. 2 HEN
- 1st movement

Sonata in F Major ("Spring"), op. 24 HEN
- 1st movement

Elsner, Józef
Sonata in F Major, op. 10, no. 1 PWM
- 2nd *and* 3rd movements

Girón, Arsenio
Sonata IV for Violin and Piano CMC
- complete

Hindemith, Paul
Sonata in E flat Major, op. 11, no. 1 OTT
- 1st movement

Leclair, Jean Marie
Sonata in D Major, op. 9 SCH
- *two* contrasting movements

McIntyre David
Sonata No. 1 for Violin and Piano (1993) CMC
- *two* contrasting movements

Mozart, Wolfgang Amadeus
Sonata in C Major, K 296 BAR; HEN
- 1st movement

Sonata in F Major, K 374d (376) BAR: HEN
- 1st movement

Sonata in F Major, K 374e (377) BAR; HEN
- 1st movement

Sonata in F Major, K376 BAR; HEN
- 3rd movement

Paganini, Nicolo
- Sonata in E Minor, op. 3, no. 12 INT

Schubert, Franz
Sonatina in A Minor, op. posth. 137, no. 2, D 385 BAR; HEN
- 1st *and* 2nd movements

Tartini, Giuseppe
Sonata in G Minor ("Didone Abbandonata"), op. 1, no. 10, Bg10 OTT; RIC
- 1st *and* 2nd movements

Veracini, Francesco Maria
Sonata in E Minor, op. 2, no. 8 INT; RIC (in *Suzuki Violin School*, 8 ALF)
- 1st *and* 2nd movements

Vivaldi, Antonio
Sonata in D Major, RV 10/F XII: 6 (transc. Ottorino Respighi RIC)
- *two* contrasting movements

Willan, Healey
Sonata No. 1 in E Minor BER; CMC
- 1st movement

List C
Concert Repertoire

Achron, Joseph
- Hebrew Melody, op. 33 FIS

Albeniz, Isaac
- Malagueña (arr. Fritz Kreisler FIS) MAS
- Mallorca, from *Three Spanish Dances* MAS
- Tango in D Major, op. 165, no. 2 INT (arr. Samuel Dushkin OTT)

Bacewicz, Grażyna
- Humoreska (in *Violinmusik von Komponistinnen* OTT)
- Polish Caprice for Violin Solo PWM

Barber, Samuel
- Canzone, op. 38 (in *Samuel Barber: Music for Violin and Piano* SCH)

Beethoven, Ludwig van
- Romance in F Major, op. 50 BAR; SCH

Bridge, Frank
- Moto Perpetuo B&H

Brahms, Johannes
- Hungarian Dance No. 5 from *Hungarian Dances* WoO 1 (arr. Joseph Joachim FIS)

Bruch, Max
- Kol Nidre, op. 47 FIS

Copland, Aaron
- Vieux Poème (Old Poem) (in *Copland for Violin* B&H)

Debussy, Claude
- La plus que lent (arr. Leon Rocques DUR)

Dvořák, Antonín

- Slavonic Dance No. 1 in G Minor, arr. from op. 46, no. 2 and op. 72, no. 1 (arr. Fritz Kreisler, in *The Fritz Kreisler Collection*, 2 FIS)
- Slavonic Dance No. 3 in G Major, from op. 72, no. 8 (arr. Fritz Kreisler in *The Fritz Kreisler Collection*, 2 FIS)

Romantic Pieces, op. 75 BAR; HEN

- *two* pieces

Eckhardt-Gramatté, Sophie-Carmen

Ten Caprices CMC

- Caprice No. 1

Godowsky, Leopold

- Alt-Wien, from *Triakontameron* (arr. Jascha Heifetz FIS)

Gratton, Hector

- Quatrième danse canadienne BER; CMC

Holt, Patricia Blomfield

Suite No. 2 BER; CMC

- *two* contrasting movements

Hubay, Jenö

- Hejre Kati (Scènes de la Csárda no. 4), op. 32 SCH; FIS

Kreisler, Fritz

- Romance, op. 4 MAS

Moszkowski, Moritz

Spanische Tänze, op. 12

- Spanischer Tänz (no. 5)

Mozart, Wolfgang Amadeus

- Rondo in C Major, K 373 BAR; INT

Rachmaninoff, Sergei

- Vocalise, op. 34, no. 14 INT (in *Solos for Young Violinists*, 6 ALF)

Sarasate, Pablo de

- Malagueña (*Danse espagnole*, op. 21, no. 1) INT

Shostakovich, Dmitri

Nine Preludes, op. 34

- *two* contrasting nos. 1, 2, 5, 6, 8, 9

Stravinsky, Igor

- Ballad, from *The Fairy's Kiss* B&H

Suk, Joseph

Four Pieces, op. 17 ALF; SIM

- *one* piece

Svendsen, Johan

- Romance, op. 26 PET; FIS

Tchaikovsky, Pyotr Il'yich

- Mélodie, op. 42, no. 3 FIS; INT

List D
Unaccompanied Repertoire of Johann Sebastian Bach

Bach, Johann Sebastian

Partita No. 1 in B Minor, BWV 1002 BAR; HEN

- Courante

Partita No. 2 in D Minor, BWV 1004 BAR; HEN

- Allemande
- Corrente
- Sarabanda

Partita No. 3 in E Major, BWV 1006 BAR; HEN

- Gavotte en rondeau
- Loure

Sonata No. 1 in G Minor, BWV 1001 BAR; HEN

- Siciliana

Sonata No. 3 in C Major, BWV 1005 BAR; HEN

- Allegro assai

Orchestral Excerpts

Candidates should be prepared to play the first violin part of *two* contrasting excerpts by two different composers from the following list. Candidates are encouraged to listen to and become familiar with the works from which these excerpts are taken. The candidate's ability to perform excerpts in a manner that demonstrates an understanding of the style and context is an important examination criterion. For instructions regarding the performance of chords please see p. 11.

- All orchestral excerpts are included in *Violin Series, 2013 Edition: Orchestral Excerpts* FHM.
- Alternatively, candidates may use standard published orchestral parts for the specific excerpts. The list below includes measure numbers for reference.

Each bulleted item (▶) represents one selection for examination purposes.

Beethoven, Ludwig van

String Quartet No. 4 in C Minor, op. 18

▶ 4th movement: pickup to mm. 41–86

Symphony No. 1 in C Major, op. 21

▶ 3rd movement: mm. 1–103 *and* 4th movement: mm. 1–47 (first sixteenth note)

Britten, Benjamin

The Young Person's Guide to the Orchestra: Variations and Fugue on a Theme of Henry Purcell, op. 34

▶ Variation M: mm. 1–54

Dvořák, Antonín

Serenade for Strings in E Major, op. 22

▶ 2nd movement: pickup to mm. 1–46, pickup to mm. 80–158

Haydn, Franz Joseph
Symphony No. 104 in D Major, Hob. I:104 ("London")
- ▶ 1st movement: mm. 17–64 *and* 2nd movement: mm. 1–8, 42–56

Mozart, Wolfgang Amadeus
Symphony No. 40 in G Minor, K 550
- ▶ 1st movement: mm. 1–42 *and* 4th movement: mm. 1–48

Rossini, Gioachino
La gazza ladra
- ▶ Overture: pickup to mm. 4–11, pickup to mm. 42–49, 62–114

Technical Requirements

Please see "Technical Requirements" on p. 11 for important information regarding this section of the examination.

Etudes

Candidates must prepare *one* etude from the following list. Each bulleted item (●) represents one selection for examination purposes.

Campagnoli, Bartolomeo
7 Divertimenti, op. 18 RIC; KMA
Divertimento No. 1
- ● Siciliano
- ● Menuetto and Trio

Divertimento No. 3
- ● Allemande

Dont, Jacob
Twenty-four Exercises, op. 37 INT; SCH
- ● *one* of nos. 13–24

Dancla, Charles
20 Études brillantes et caractéristiques, op. 73 EMB
- ● no. 4 *or* no. 8

Fiorillo, Federigo
36 Etudes or Caprices INT; SCH
- ● *one* of nos. 7, 21, 22, 31

Kreutzer, Rodolphe
Quarante-deux études ou caprices INT
- ● *one* of nos. 18–26

Rode, Pierre
24 Caprices FIS; INT
- ● *one* of nos. 1–3, 5, 8, 10

Technical Tests

Please see "Technical Tests" on p. 11 for important information regarding this section of the examination.

Candidates must play all scales, arpeggios, and double stops from memory.

Scales	Keys	Range	Tempo	Bowing
Major	E♭, E, F	3 octaves	♩ = 84	
Harmonic and Melodic Minor	E♭, E, F			
Major Artificial Harmonics	G, A	2 octaves	♩ = 84	
Chromatic	on B, on C, on D	3 octaves	♩ = 72	
Arpeggios				
Major	E♭, E, F	3 octaves	♩. = 92	
Minor	E♭, E, F			
Dominant 7th of Major Keys	G♭ (starting on D♭), G (starting on D), A♭ (starting on E♭)	3 octaves	♩ = 60	
Diminished 7th of Minor Keys	D (starting on C♯), E♭ (starting on D♮), E (starting on D♯)	3 octaves	♩ = 60	
Double Stops				
Major in 3rds, 6ths, 8ves	B♭, C	2 octaves	♩ = 84	
Harmonic and Melodic Minor in 3rds, 6ths, 8ves	B♭, C			

Ear Tests

Intervals

Candidates will be asked to identify the following intervals. The examiner will play each interval *once* in broken form on the piano.

or

Candidates may choose to sing or hum the following intervals. The examiner will play the first note *once* on the piano.

Above a Given Note	Below a Given Note
any interval within the octave	any interval within the octave *except* the augmented 4th/diminished 5th

Chords

Candidates will be asked to identify the following chords and their inversion or position after the examiner has played the chord *once* in solid (blocked) form, close position on the piano.

Chords	Position
major and minor triads	root position, 1st inversion
dominant 7th	root position
diminished 7th	root position

Cadences

Candidates will be asked to identify the following cadences by name or symbols. The examiner will play the tonic chord *once,* and then *twice* play a short phrase ending in a cadence.

Name of Cadence	Symbols
perfect or authentic	V–I
plagal	IV–I
imperfect	I–V

Example only

Playback

Candidates will be asked to play back the upper part of a two-part phrase on the violin. The examiner will name the key, play the tonic triad *once,* and play the phrase *twice* on the piano.

Beginning Note	Keys	Approximate Length
tonic, mediant, dominant, or upper tonic	any major key	two or three measures

Example only

Sight Reading

Playing

Candidates will be asked to play a short melody at sight. New features introduced at Grade 9 may include turns, thirty-second notes, and *restez* position indications.

Difficulty	Time Signatures	Keys	Positions	Approximate Length
Grade 7 repertoire	2/4 3/4 4/4 5/4 3/8 6/8 ¢	C, F, B♭, E♭, G, D, A, E major A, D, G, E, B, C♯ minor	1st to 6th	sixteen to twenty measures

Clapping

Candidates will be asked to clap or tap the rhythm of a melody. A steady pulse and rhythmic precision are expected.

Time Signatures	Approximate Length
2/4 3/4 4/4 6/8	four to six measures

Example only

Grade 10

Candidates in Grade 10 should be able to execute all bow strokes and maintain control and security in any position. Intonation should be precise. Tone should be mature and soloistic, with an expressive and varied vibrato. Playing should be sophisticated, nuanced, and stylistically aware.

Grade 10 candidates who wish to pursue an ARCT in Violin Performance or a Teacher's ARCT must achieve either an overall mark of 75 or a minimum of 70 percent in each section of the Grade 10 examination. Figures in bold parentheses indicate the minimum number of marks required to receive the equivalent of 70 percent.

Grade 10 Requirements	Marks
Repertoire	**50 (35)**
one selection from List A	15 (1.5)
one selection from List B	15
one selection from List C	10 (1)
one selection from List D	10 (1)
(The figures in parentheses for Lists A, C, and D indicate the marks that will be deducted for selections that are not memorized.)	
Orchestral Excerpts	**10 (7)**
two contrasting excerpts from the *Syllabus* list	
Technical Requirements	**20 (14)**
Etudes: *one* etude from the *Syllabus* list	8
Technical Tests	12
– scales	
– arpeggios	
– double stops	
Ear Tests	**10 (7)**
Intervals	2
Chords	2
Cadences	3
Playback	3
Sight Reading	**10 (7)**
Playing	7
Clapping	3
Total possible marks (pass = 60)	**100**
Theory Co-requisites	
Advanced Rudiments	
Intermediate Harmony *or* Intermediate Keyboard Harmony	
History 1: An Overview	
History 2: Middle Ages to Classical	

Please see "Co-requisites and Prerequisites" on p. 8, "Classification of Marks" on p. 81, and "Supplemental Examinations" on p. 83 for important details regarding Grade 10 standing for an ARCT examination application.

Repertoire

Please see "Examination Repertoire" on p. 9 for important information regarding this section of the examination.

Candidates must prepare *four* contrasting selections: *one* from List A, *one* from List B, *one* from List C, and *one* from List D. Candidates are encouraged to select repertoire in a variety of keys and tempos, with no more than two works from the same era (for example, only two selections from the Baroque era).

Each bulleted item (●) represents one selection for examination purposes.

Please note that *cadenzas* are required where indicated. Unless otherwise indicated, any *cadenza* is acceptable, as long as the examiner is provided with an original copy of the music, and it is equivalent in difficulty to the standard *cadenza* for that work.

List A

Concertos

Barber, Samuel
Concerto, op. 14 SCH
- 1st movement (with *cadenza*) *and* 2nd movement

Bruch, Max
Concerto in G Minor, op. 26 PET; SCH; INT
- 1st *and* 2nd movements
- 2nd *and* 3rd movements

Kabalevsky, Dmitri
Concerto in C Major, op. 48 INT
- 1st *and* 2nd movements
- 2nd movement *and* 3rd movement (complete)

Khachaturian, Aram
Concerto in D Minor B&H
- 1st *and* 2nd movements
- 2nd *and* 3rd movements

Lalo, Edouard
Symphonie espagnole, op. 21 SCH
- 2nd *and* 3rd movements

Mozart, Wolfgang Amadeus
Concerto in D Major, K 218 BAR; INT
- 1st movement (with *cadenza*) *and* 2nd movement (with *cadenza*)

Spohr, Louis
Concerto No. 2 in D Minor, op. 2 PET
- 1st *and* 2nd movements

Concerto No. 9 in D Minor, op. 55 PET
- 1st *and* 2nd movements

Viotti, Giovanni Battista
Concerto No. 22 in A Minor SCH
- 1st movement (with *cadenza*) *and* 2nd movement (with *cadenza*)

List B
Sonatas

Beethoven, Ludwig van
Sonata in A Minor, op. 23 HEN
- 1st *and* 2nd movements

Sonata in A Major, op. 30, no. 1 HEN
- 1st *and* 2nd movements

Sonata in G Major, op. 30, no. 3 HEN
- 1st *and* 2nd movements

Sonata in G Major, op. 96 HEN
- 1st *and* 2nd movements

Brahms, Johannes
Sonata in A Major, op. 100 HEN; INT
- 1st *and* 2nd movements

Sonata in G Major, op. 78 HEN; INT
- 1st *and* 2nd movements

Buczynski, Walter
Sonata (1979) CMC
- complete

Girón, Arsenio
Sonata breve CMC
- 1st *and* 2nd movements
- 3rd *and* 4th movements

Grieg, Edvard
Sonata in F Major, op. 8, no. 1 PET; SCH
- 1st *and* 2nd movements

Sonata in C Minor, op. 45, no. 3 PET; SCH
- 1st *and* 2nd movements

Hindemith, Paul
Sonata in C Major (1939) OTT
- 1st *and* 2nd movements

Mozart, Wolfgang Amadeus
Sonata in E flat Major, K 481 BAR; HEN
- 1st movement

Sonata in A Major, K 526 BAR; HEN
- 1st *and* 2nd movements

Prokofiev, Sergei
Sonata, op. 115 PET
- 1st *and* 2nd movements
- 2nd *and* 3rd movements

Schubert, Franz
Sonata in A Major, op. posth. 162, D 574 BAR; HEN; OTT
- 1st *and* 2nd movements

Schumann, Robert
Sonata in A Minor, op. 105, no. 1 PET
- 1st *and* 2nd movements

Vallerand, Jean
Sonata (1950) DOM; CMC
- *two* contrasting movements

List C
Concert Repertoire

Anonymous
- Ciaccona in G Minor (attr. Tomaso Antonio Vitali) (ed. Diethard Hellmann BAR; arr. Léopold Charlier FIS; arr. Leopold Auer FIS)

Adaskin, Murray
- Canzona and Rondo CMC

Archer, Violet
- Prelude and Allegro BER; CMC

Baker, Michael Conway
- The Flight of Aphrodite, op. 99 CMC

Bartók, Béla
- Hungarian Folk Songs (transc. Tivadar Országh EMB)
- Roumanian Folk Dances UNI (in *Solos for Young Violinists*, 6 ALF)

Bax, Arnold
- Legend MAS

Beethoven, Ludwig van
- Romance in G Major, op. 40 BAR; HEN

Bériot, Charles-Auguste de
- Scène de Ballet, op. 100 SCH; FIS

Bloch, Ernest
- Nigun, from *Baal Shem* FIS

Boulanger, Lili
- D'un matin de printemps FAB, SCH

Brahms, Johannes
Hungarian Dances WoO 1 (arr. Joseph Joachim FIS)
- *one* of nos. 1, 2, 3

Chan, Ka Nin
- Soulmate for Solo Violin CMC

Copland, Aaron
- Hoe-down, from *Rodeo* B&H

Debussy, Claude
- Golliwogg's Cake-walk (arr. Jascha Heifetz, in *The Heifetz Collection,* 1 FIS)

Dvořák, Antonín
- Romance in F Minor, op. 11 INT, SCH
- Slavonic Dance in E Minor, op. 46, no. 2 (arr. Fritz Kreisler FIS)

Eckhardt-Gramatté, Sophie-Carmen
Ten Caprices CMC
- Caprice No. 2
- Caprice No. 3

Girón, Arsenio
Five Episodes CMC
- *three* contrasting movements

Kreisler, Fritz
- Praeludium and Allegro (in the Style of Pugnani) OTT; FIS
- Variations on a Theme of Corelli (in the Style of Giuseppe Tartini) OTT; FIS

Kroll, William
- Banjo and Fiddle SCH

Lau, Kevin
- Joy CMC

Moszkowski, Moritz
- Guitarre, op. 45, no. 2 FIS; PET

Mozart, Wolfgang Amadeus
- Rondo in G Major, from *Haffner Serenade*, K 250 (arr. Fritz Kreisler OTT; FIS)

Novácek, Ottokar
- Moto perpetuo INT

Prokofiev, Sergei
- Five Melodies, op. 35 bis B&H
- March from *Love for Three Oranges* (arr. Jascha Heifetz FIS)

Sarasate, Pablo de
- Romanza Andaluza (*Danse espagnole,* op. 22, no. 1) INT

Schumann, Robert
- Dedication (in *Auer Selected Pieces* MUZ)

Sinding, Christian
Suite in A Minor, op. 10 INT
- 1st *and* 2nd movements
- 3rd *and* 4th movements

Tchaikovsky, Pyotr Il'yich
- Scherzo, op. 42, no. 2 PET
- Sérénade mélancolique, op. 26 PET

Webern, Anton von
- Four Pieces, op. 7 UNI

Wieniawski, Henryk
- Légende, op. 17 FIS

List D
Unaccompanied Repertoire of Johann Sebastian Bach

Bach, Johann Sebastian
Partita No. 1 in B Minor, BWV 1002 BAR; HEN
- Allemande *and* Double
- Sarabande *and* Double
- Tempo di bourrée *and* Double

Partita No. 3 in E Major, BWV 1006 BAR; HEN
- Preludio

Sonata No. 1 in G Minor, BWV 1001 BAR; HEN
- Adagio
- Presto

Sonata No. 2 in A Minor, BWV 1003 BAR; HEN; INT
- Andante
- Allegro

Sonata No. 3 in C Major, BWV 1005 BAR; HEN; INT
- Adagio
- Largo

Orchestral Excerpts

Candidates should be prepared to play the first violin part of *two* contrasting excerpts by two different composers from the following list. Candidates are encouraged to listen to and become familiar with the works from which these excerpts are taken. The candidate's ability to perform excerpts in a manner that demonstrates an understanding of the style and context is an important examination criterion. For instructions regarding the performance of chords please see p. 11.

- All orchestral excerpts are included in *Violin Series, 2013 Edition: Orchestral Excerpts* FHM.
- Alternatively, candidates may use standard published orchestral parts for the specific excerpts. The list below includes measure numbers for reference.

Each bulleted item (▶) represents one selection for examination purposes.

Beethoven, Ludwig van
Symphony No. 9 in D Minor, op. 125
- ▶ 2nd movement: mm. 21–93 (beat 1) *and* 3rd movement: mm. 99–114

Berlioz, Hector
Symphonie fantastique, op. 14
- ▶ 1st movement (*Rêveries, passions*): mm. 3–24 *and* 2nd movement (*Un bal*): pickup to mm. 39–94 (first sixteenth note), pickup to mm. 257–302

Brahms, Johannes
Symphony No. 1 in C Minor, op. 68
- ▶ 1st movement: mm. 1–29, 41–70

Dvořák, Antonín
String Quartet No. 12 in F Major ("American"), op. 96
- ▶ 1st movement: pickup to mm. 112–152 (beat 1)

Mendelssohn, Felix
Symphony No. 4 in A Major ("Italian"), op. 90
- ▶ 1st movement: mm. 1–110

Mozart, Wolfgang Amadeus
Die Zauberflöte, K 620
- ▶ Overture: mm. 20–96, 216–end

Tchaikovsky, Pyotr Il'yich
Serenade for Strings, op. 48
- ▶ 1st movement: mm. 1–36, 91–138

Symphony No. 4 in F Minor, op. 36
- ▶ 1st movement: pickup to mm. 70–103 *and* 2nd movement: mm. 85–117 *and* 4th movement: mm. 30–59

Weber, Carl Maria von
Oberon, J 306
- ▶ Overture: mm. 11–16, pickup to mm. 23–55, 117–145

Technical Requirements

Please see "Technical Requirements" on p. 11 for important information regarding this section of the examination.

Etudes

Candidates must prepare *one* etude from the following list. Each bulleted item (●) represents one selection for examination purposes.

Campagnoli, Bartolomeo
7 Divertimenti, op 18 RIC; KMH
Divertimento No. 4
- ● Bolero
- ● Finale

Divertimento No. 5
- ● Allegro

Divertimento No. 6
- ● Finale

Dont, Jacob
Etudes and Caprices, op. 35 SCH; INT
- ● any *one*

Dancla, Charles
20 Études brillantes et caractéristiques, op. 73 EMB
- ● no. 6 *or* no. 16

Gaviniès, Pierre
24 Études (Matinées) PET; INT
- ● any *one*

Kreutzer, Rodolphe
Quarante-deux études ou caprices INT
- ● *one* of nos. 27–42

Locatelli, Pietro
The Art of the Violin: 24 Caprices for Solo Violin, op. 3 RIC
- ● any *one*

Rode, Pierre
24 Caprices FIS; INT
- ● *one* of nos. 4, 6, 7, 9, 11–24

Rovelli, Pietro
12 Caprices, op. 3 IMS
- ● any *one*

Technical Tests

Please see "Technical Tests" on p. 11 for important information regarding this section of the examination.

Candidates must play all scales, arpeggios, and double stops from memory.

Scales	Keys	Range	Tempo	Bowing
Major	all keys	3 octaves	♩ = 90	
Harmonic and Melodic Minor	all keys			
Major Artificial Harmonics	B♭	2 octaves	♩ = 84	
Harmonic and Melodic Minor Artificial Harmonics	B♭			
Chromatic	on any note	3 octaves	♩ = 84	
Arpeggios				
Major	all keys	3 octaves	♩. = 108	
Minor	all keys			
Dominant 7th of Major Keys	all keys	3 octaves	♩ = 72	
Diminished 7th of Minor Keys	all keys	3 octaves	♩ = 72	
Double Stops				
Major in 3rds, 6ths, 8ves	D, E, F	2 octaves	♩ = 104	
Harmonic and Melodic Minor in 3rds, 6ths, 8ves	D, E, F			
Major in Solid Fingered 8ves	one key (student's choice)	1 octave alternate 1–3 and 2–4 fingering	♩ = 104	
Major in Solid 10ths	one key (student's choice)	1 octave on A and E strings	♩ = 104	

Ear Tests

Intervals

Candidates will be asked to identify the following intervals. The examiner will play each interval *once* in broken form on the piano.
or
Candidates may choose to sing or hum the following intervals. The examiner will play the first note *once* on the piano.

Above a Given Note	Below a Given Note
any interval within the octave	any interval within the octave

Chords

Candidates will be asked to identify the following chords and their inversion or position after the examiner has played the chord *once* in solid (blocked) form, close position on the piano.

Chords	Position
major and minor four-note chords	root position, 1st inversion, 2nd inversion
dominant 7th	root position
diminished 7th	root position

Cadences

Candidates will be asked to identify by name or symbols the following cadences played within a single phrase. The phrase may be in a major or minor key and may contain up to three cadences. The examiner will play the tonic chord *once*, then play the phrase *twice*.

Name of Cadence	Symbols
perfect or authentic	V(7)–I
plagal	IV–I
imperfect	I –V
deceptive (interrupted)	V (7)–VI

Example only

Playback

Candidates will be asked to play back the lower part of a two-part phrase on the violin. The examiner will name the key, play the tonic triad *once*, and play the phrase *twice* on the piano.

Beginning Note	Keys	Approximate Length
Tonic, mediant, dominant, or upper tonic	any major key	two to four measures

Example only

Sight Reading

Playing

Candidates will be asked to play a short melody at sight. New features introduced at Grade 10 may include *cadenza*-like passages, double sharps, double flats, and changes of meter.

Difficulty	Time Signatures	Keys	Positions	Approximate Length
Grade 8 repertoire	2/4 3/4 4/4 5/4 3/8 6/8 ¢	any major or minor key	any position, including *sul* string option	sixteen to twenty measures

Clapping

Candidates will be asked to clap or tap the rhythm of a melody. A steady pulse and rhythmic precision are expected.

Time Signatures	Approximate Length
2/4 3/4 4/4 6/8	four to six measures

Example only

ARCT in Violin Performance

The ARCT in Violin Performance is the culmination of The Royal Conservatory Examinations Certificate Program, and is evaluated as a concert performance. Excellence in every aspect of performance is expected. Candidates are expected to perform with confidence, communicating the essence of the music while demonstrating a command of the instrument. A detailed understanding of the stylistic and structural elements of each repertoire selection is expected. Candidates must achieve an Honors standing (70 percent) in order to be awarded an ARCT in Violin Performance Diploma.

For descriptions of performance marks, please see "Marking Criteria for Performance of Repertoire" on p. 81. An ARCT candidate's performance of a work may receive a failing grade for any of the following reasons:

- repeated breaks in continuity
- substantial omissions
- lack of technical control
- textual inaccuracies
- inappropriate tempo, character, or style

The ARCT Examination

Please see "Co-requisites and Prerequisites" on p. 8, "Classification of Marks" on p. 81, and "Supplemental Examinations" on p. 83 for important details regarding the ARCT in Violin Performance examination. Candidates are strongly recommended to study for at least two years after passing the Grade 10 examination.

ARCT in Violin Performance Requirements	Marks
Repertoire	**80**
one selection from List A	20 (2)
one selection from List B	20
one selection from List C	20 (2)
one selection from List D	20 (2)
(The figures in parentheses for Lists A, C, and D indicate the marks that will be deducted for selections that are not memorized.)	
Orchestral Excerpts	**20**
two excerpts from the *Syllabus* list	
– *one* from List 1 (Orchestral *Tutti* Parts)	10
– *one* from List 2 (Concertmaster Solos and Chamber Music Repertoire)	10
Total possible marks (pass = 70)	**100**
Theory Prerequisites	
Advanced Rudiments	
Intermediate Harmony *or* Intermediate Keyboard Harmony	
History 1: An Overview	
History 2: Middle Ages to Classical	
Theory Co-requisites	
History 3: 19th Century to Present	
And any *two* of:	
Advanced Harmony *or* Advanced Keyboard Harmony	
Counterpoint	
Analysis	
Piano Co-requisite	
Grade 6 Piano	

Repertoire

Please see "Examination Repertoire" on p. 9 for important information regarding this section of the examination.

Candidates must prepare *four* contrasting selections by four different composers: *one* from List A, *one* from List B, *one* from List C, and *one* from List D. Candidates are expected to select repertoire in a variety of keys and tempos, representing at least three different historical eras.

Each bulleted item (●) represents one selection for examination purposes. Unless otherwise indicated, candidates should prepare the complete work. *Note that the selections in List B need not be memorized.*

The length of the performance must be between 40 and 50 minutes. The examiner may stop the performance if it exceeds the allotted time.

Please note that *cadenzas* are required where indicated in the score. In general, any *cadenza* is acceptable, as long as the examiner is provided with an original copy of the music, and it is equivalent in difficulty to the standard *cadenza* for that work.

List A
Concertos and Fantasias

Bruch, Max
Concerto in D Minor, op. 44, no. 2 FIS
- 1st *and* 2nd movements

Scottish Fantasy in E flat Major, op. 46 SCH; INT
- 1st *and* 2nd movements
- 3rd *and* 4th movements

Conus, Jules
Concerto in E Minor FIS; MAS; INT
- 1st *and* 2nd movements

Dvořák, Antonín
Concerto in A Minor, op. 53 BAR; INT
- 1st *and* 2nd movements
- 2nd *and* 3rd movements

Lalo, Édouard
Symphonie espagnole, op. 21 HEN; SCH
- 1st *and* 4th movements
- 4th *and* 5th movements

Mendelssohn, Felix
Concerto in E Minor, op. 64 BAR; FIS; PET
- 1st *and* 2nd movements
- 2nd *and* 3rd movements

Mozart, Wolfgang Amadeus
Concerto in A Major, K 219 INT; BAR
- 1st and 2nd movements

Paganini, Niccolò
Concerto No. 1 in D Major, op. 6 SIM; INT
- 1st *and* 2nd movements

Mozetich, Marjan
- Affairs of the Heart CMC

Po, Liang Shan and Zhu Ying Tai
- Butterfly Lover's Concerto (arr. Guan Sheng You)

Prokofiev, Sergei
Concerto No. 1 in D Major, op. 19 INT
- 1st *and* 2nd movements

Concerto No. 2 in G Minor, op. 63 INT
- 1st *and* 2nd movements

Saint-Saëns, Camille
Concerto in B Minor, op. 61 SCH; INT
- 1st *and* 2nd movements
- 2nd *and* 3rd movements

Tchaikovsky, Pyotr Il'yich
Concerto in D Major, op. 35 HEN; INT; OTT; BOS; KAL
- 1st movement (with *cadenza*)
- 2nd *and* 3rd movements

Vieuxtemps, Henri
Concerto No. 4 in D Minor, op. 31 FIS; INT
- 1st *and* 2nd movements

Concerto No. 5 in A Minor, op. 37 PET; INT
- 1st *and* 2nd movements

Weinzweig, John
Concerto CMC
- 1st *and* 2nd movements

Wieniawski, Henryk
Concerto in D Minor, op. 22 PET; INT
- 1st *and* 2nd movements
- 2nd and 3rd movements

List B
Sonatas

Adaskin, Murray
Sonata No. 1 (1946) CMC
- 1st *and* 2nd movements

Beethoven, Ludwig van
Sonata in C Minor, op. 30, no. 2 HEN
- *two* contrasting movements

Sonata in E flat Major, op. 12, no. 3 HEN
- 1st *and* 2nd movements

Brahms, Johannes
Sonata in D Minor, op. 108 INT
- *two* contrasting movements

Coulthard, Jean
- Duo Sonata BER; CMC

Debussy, Claude
Sonata in G Minor DUR; PET
- *two* contrasting movements

Dolin, Samuel
Sonata BER; CMC
- *two* contrasting movements

Dvořák, Antonín
Sonata in F Major, op. 57 BAR
- *two* contrasting movements

Fauré, Gabriel
Sonata in A Major, op. 13 HEN; SCH; INT
- *two* contrasting movements

Franck, César
Sonata in A Major HEN; SCH
- *two* contrasting movements

Girón, Arsenio
- Violin Sonata II (Three Invitations) CMC

Grieg, Edvard
Sonata in G Major, op. 13 (1867) PET; FIS
- 1st *and* 2nd movements

Hindemith, Paul
Sonata in D Major, op. 11, no. 2 OTT
- 1st *and* 2nd movements

MacDonald, Andrew P.
Violin Sonata No. 2 ("The Phœnix") CMC
- 1st movement
- 2nd movement

Morawetz, Oskar
- Duo RIC; CMC
- Sonata no. 1 (1956) AEN; CMC

Mozart, Wolfgang Amadeus
Sonata in B flat Major, K 454 BAR; HEN
- *two* contrasting movements

Prokofiev, Sergei
Sonata in D Major, op. 94a INT
- *two* contrasting movements

Raum, Elizabeth
- Sonata CMC

Respighi, Ottorino
Sonata in B Minor RIC
- *two* contrasting movements

Somers, Harry
Sonata No. 2 BER; CMC
- *two* contrasting movements

Strauss, Richard
Sonata in E flat Major, op. 18 UNI
- *two* contrasting movements

Stravinsky, Igor
Duo concertante B&H
- *two* contrasting movements

Tartini, Giuseppe
Sonata G Minor ("Devil's Trill") Bg5 OTT; RIC
- *two* contrasting movements (with *cadenza*)

Weinzweig, John
- Sonata OUP; CMC

List C
Concert Repertoire

Andrzejowski, Umińska
- Burleska PWM

Bartók, Béla
- Rhapsody No. 1 B&H

Berlioz, Hector
- Rêverie et caprice (Romance) BAR

Brott, Alexander
- Invocation and Dance CMC

Dinicu, Grigora
- Hora Staccato (Roumanian) (arr. Jascha Heifetz FIS)

Elgar, Edward
- La capricieuse, op. 17 FIS; BRH

Falla, Manuel de
- Danse espagnole, from *La vida breve* (arr. Fritz Kreisler FIS)

Kabalevsky, Dmitri
- Rondo, op. 69 MAS

Kreisler, Fritz
- Caprice viennois, op. 2 FIS
- Recitative and Scherzo caprice FIS
- Tambourin chinois, op. 3 FIS

Mozetich, Marjan
- L'esprit chantant CMC

Paganini, Niccolò
- Moto Perpetuo INT

Papineau-Couture, Jean
Trois caprices PER; CMC
- *two* contrasting movements

Pentland, Barbara
- Vista BER; CMC

Piazzolla, Astor
- Le Grand Tango BEB

Raum, Elizabeth
- Les ombres CMC
- Prayer and Dance of Praise CMC

Ravel, Maurice
- Tzigane BAR; DUR

Robinovitch, Sid
- Meditation CMC

Saint-Saëns, Camille
- Havanaise, op. 83 BAR; FIS; SCH; INT
- Introduction and Rondo capriccioso, op. 28 FIS; SCH; INT

Sarasate, Pablo de
- Habañera (*Danse espagnole,* op. 21, no. 2) INT
- Introduction and Tarantelle, op. 43 INT
- Zapateado (*Danse espagnole,* op. 23, no. 2) INT; EMB
- Zigeunerweisen, op. 20 FIS; INT

Stravinsky, Igor
Suite Italienne B&H
- 1st, 3rd, *and* 6th movements

Szymanowski, Karol
- La fontaine d'Aréthuse, op. 30, no. 1 PWM
- Nocturne and Tarentella, op. 28, no. 1 UNI; INT

Tchaikovsky, Pyotr Il'yich
- Meditation, op. 42, no. 1 FIS; INT
- Waltz-Scherzo, op. 34 INT

Vaughan Williams, Ralph
- The Lark Ascending OUP

Vieuxtemps, Henri
- Rondino op. 32, no. 2 (in *Masterpieces for Violin* FIS)

Wieniawski, Henryk
- Polonaise brillante in A Major, op. 21 INT; SCH
- Polonaise in D Major, op. 4 INT
- Scherzo tarantella in G Minor, op. 16 PET; FIS

Zarzycki, Aleksander
- Mazurka in G Major, op. 26 PWM

List D
Unaccompanied Repertoire

Bach, Johann Sebastian
Partita No. 2 in D Minor, BWV 1004 BAR; HEN
- Chaconne

Sonata No. 1 in G Minor, BWV 1001 BAR; HEN
- Fugue

Sonata No. 2 in A Minor, BWV 1003 BAR; HEN
- Fugue

Sonata No. 3 in C Major, BWV 1005 BAR; HEN
- Fugue

Eckhardt-Gramatté, Sophie-Carmen
Ten Caprices CMC
- *one* of nos. 5–10

Gruber, H.K.
- Four Pieces for Solo Violin B&H

Hétu, Jacques
- Rondo varié pour violon seul, op. 25 DOM; CMC
- Variations, op. 11 DOM; CMC

Ledroit, Christien
- Wandering the Threshold of Delirium CMC (to be performed without audio track)

Paganini, Niccolò
Twenty-Four Caprices, op. 1 EMB
- *one* of nos. 9, 13, 14, 16, 18, 20

Prévost, André
- Improvisations I pour Violine Seul DOM; CMC

Ysaÿe, Eugène
Six Sonatas, op. 27 SCH
Sonata No. 1
- *two* contrasting movements

Sonata No. 3
- complete

Sonata No. 6
- complete

Zarzycki, Aleksander
- Mazurka in G Major, op. 26 PWM

Orchestral Excerpts

Candidates should be prepared to play *two* excerpts by different composers: *one* from Group 1 and *one* from Group 2. Candidates are encouraged to listen to and become familiar with the works from which these excerpts are taken. The candidate's ability to perform excerpts in a manner that demonstrates an understanding of the style and context is an important examination criterion. For instructions regarding the performance of chords please see p. 11.

- All orchestral excerpts are included in *Violin Series, 2013 Edition: Orchestral Excerpts* FHM.
- Alternatively, candidates may use standard published orchestral parts for the specific excerpts. The list below includes measure numbers for reference.

Each bulleted item (▶) represents one selection for examination purposes.

Group 1
Orchestral *Tutti* Parts (First Violin)

Brahms, Johannes
Symphony No. 4 in E Minor, op. 98
- ▶ 4th movement: mm. 41–80, 153–177

Mendelssohn, Felix
Incidental Music to *A Midsummer Night's Dream,* op. 21
- ▶ 1st movement (Scherzo): mm. 17–99, 115–135

Mozart, Wolfgang Amadeus
Symphony No. 39 in E flat Major, K 54
- ▶ 1st movement: mm. 1–16, 26–90 *and* 4th movement: pickup to mm. 1–78

Prokofiev, Sergei
Symphony No. 1 ("Classical"), op. 25
- ▶ 1st movement: mm. 1–32 *and* 2nd movement: mm. 1–20 (beat 1) *and* 4th movement: mm. 1–41, 129–162

Schumann, Robert
Symphony No. 2 in C Major, op. 61
- ▶ 2nd movement (Scherzo): pickup to mm. 1–97

Shostakovich, Dmitri
Symphony No. 5, op. 47
- ▶ 1st movement: mm. 254–277 (beat 1)

Smetana, Bedřich
The Bartered Bride
- ▶ Overture: mm. 1–14, 31–66 (beat 2), 401–421 (beat 1)

Strauss, Richard
Don Juan, op. 20
- ▶ mm. 1–62

Group 2
Concertmaster Solos and Chamber Music Repertoire

Beethoven, Ludwig van
Missa solemnis, op. 123
- ▶ Sanctus (Benedictus): mm. 110–134, 140–184

Rimsky-Korsakov, Nicolai
Capriccio espagnol, op. 34
- ▶ 1st movement (Alborada): mm. 55–72 *and* 3rd movement (Alborada): mm. 14–27, 41–63 *and* 4th movement (Scena e canto gitano): solo *cadenza and* 5th movement (Fandano asturiano): mm. 25–36, 51–61

Schéhérazade, op. 35
- ▶ 1st movement: mm. 14–18, 94–102 (beat 1) *and* 3rd movement: mm. 142–165 *and* 4th movement: mm. 8–9, 29–30 (*cadenza*)

Schoenberg, Arnold
Verklärte Nacht, op. 4
- ▶ mm. 278–294, 300–318

Schubert, Franz
String Quartet No. 14 in D Minor ("Death and the Maiden"), D 810
- ▶ 1st movement: mm. 1–14, 61–114 (beat 1) *and* 4th movement: mm. 687–end

Strauss, Richard
Le Bourgeois Gentilhomme Suite, op. 60
- ▶ 4th movement (Auftritt und Tanz der Schneider): pickup to mm. 35–56, pickup to mm. 81–119

Tchaikovsky, Pyotr Il'yich
Swan Lake Suite
- ▶ 4th movement (Scène): mm. 10–34, 42–57, 65–72

Teacher's ARCT

For current information on the Teacher's ARCT requirements, please visit www.rcmusic.ca.

Register for an Examination

Login at rcmusic.ca to register.

Examination Sessions and Registration Deadlines

Exact dates and deadlines can be found online. Register early to avoid disappointment. Late registrations are subject to an additional fee and may be denied.

Winter Session—register by early November
- practical examinations take place in January
- theory examinations take place in December

Spring Session—register by early March
- practical examinations take place in June
- theory examinations take place in May

Summer Session—register by early June
- practical examinations take place in August
- theory examinations take place in August

Online Registration

All registrations should be submitted using the online registration process. Visit www.examinations.rcmusic.ca to register.

Examination Fees

Examination fees must be paid at registration using a valid credit card. Current examinations fees may be found at www.examinations.rcmusic.ca.

Examination Centres

Examinations are conducted in more than 300 communities across North America. Each examination centre has a local Examination Centre Representative who ensures that students and teachers have a successful examination experience.

Teachers may verify their students' examination schedules by visiting www.examinations.rcmusic.ca.

All candidates may verify their examination schedules online three to four weeks after the registration deadline. Examination schedules will not be mailed.

Examination Scheduling

Examination candidates may check for their examination schedules online three to four weeks after the registration deadline.

Candidates are asked to print the "Examination Program Form" using the "Examination Scheduling" feature. The program form must be filled out by the candidate and/or teacher, and brought to the examination centre for presentation to the examiner.

Candidates who, for any reason, are unable to attend an examination should contact the Centre Representative listed on their Examination Schedule. The Centre Representative may be able to provide an alternate appointment time.

Examination Regulations

Examination Procedures

Candidates must be ready to perform at least fifteen minutes before their scheduled time. *Please note that examination times cannot be exchanged among candidates.* Please contact the The Royal Conservatory Examinations Centre Representative if you are unable to attend the examination at the assigned time.

- Although most examination centres have a tune-up room, the availability of a tune-up room cannot be guaranteed. Examination centres do not provide facilities for rehearsal with piano.
- Candidates must provide their own collaborative pianist in order for an examination to proceed. Recorded accompaniments are not permitted.
- Candidates are advised to bring an electronic tuner to the examination. The piano provided for the examination will be tuned to A440.
- Examiners are not permitted to assist candidates in tuning their instruments. A teacher or assistant should be on hand to assist candidates who cannot tune accurately.
- A music stand is available in most centres, but the availability of a music stand cannot be guaranteed.
- Photo ID may be requested before candidates are admitted to the examination room.
- Candidates are asked to list all repertoire and etudes to be performed on the Examination Program Form and bring it to the examination for presentation to the examiner.
- Candidates must provide the examiner with an original, published copy of all music to be performed at the examination.
- If the candidate is performing with music, he or she should bring two original copies to the examination, one to play from and one to give to the examiner. Collaborative pianists should play from an original, published copy of the score.
- Photocopied music is not permitted in the examination room unless the candidate has a letter of permission from the publisher or website. (Please see "Copyright and Photocopying" on p. 88).
- Recording devices and cell phones are strictly prohibited in the examination room. Electronic devices, books, notes, bags, and coats must be left in the area designated by the Centre Representative.
- Page turners and other assistants are not permitted in the examination room. Waiting areas are provided for parents, teachers, and assistants. Standing or listening outside the examination room door is prohibited.
- The candidate's performance of a repertoire selection or an etude may be interrupted at the examiner's discretion once an assessment has been made.
- The examiner will choose a representative sampling of items on the technical requirements list.

Candidates must provide their own collaborative pianist in order for an examination to proceed.

Candidates must provide the examiner with an original, published copy of all music to be performed at the examination.

Recording devices and cell phones are strictly prohibited in the examination room.

Credits and Refunds for Missed Examinations

Credits (formerly called "fee extensions") and refunds are only granted in two specific situations. Candidates who are unable to attend an examination for medical reasons or because of a scheduling conflict with a school examination are eligible to request either an examination credit for the full amount of the examination fee or a fifty percent refund of the examination fee.

All requests must be submitted by mail or fax within two weeks following the examination. Requests received after this time will be denied.

Requests for examination credits or refunds must be made to The Royal Conservatory Examinations *in writing* and be accompanied by the following documentation:

- for medical reasons: a physician's letter and the candidate's examination schedule
- for direct time conflicts with school examinations: a letter from a school official on school letterhead and the candidate's Examination Schedule

Candidates who, for any reason, are unable to attend an examination should contact the Centre Representative listed on their Examination Schedule immediately.

Examination Credit

An examination credit (formerly called a "fee extension") may be applied to the fee of a future examination. Examination credits are valid for *one year* from the date of the original scheduled examination. Examination credits can be redeemed when the candidate registers for his or her next examination. The credit will be automatically applied during the online registration process. *Please note that credits are not transferable and may not be extended beyond one year.*

Fee Refund

Candidates who know at the time they are applying for a fee extension that they will not be able to make use of a credit within the one-year time period may instead apply for a refund of fifty percent of the examination fee.

Requests for examination refunds or credits must be made to The Royal Conservatory Examinations in writing and be accompanied by the necessary documentation (see above). *All requests must be submitted by mail or by fax within two weeks following the scheduled examination date.*

Candidates with Special Needs

The Special Needs Request Form is available online at www.examinations.rcmusic.ca.

Candidates with special needs should submit a Special Needs Request Form, by mail or by fax, to The Royal Conservatory Examinations before the registration deadline. Each case will be assessed individually.

Candidates may receive help in and out of the examination room if required. Please note that helpers must normally remain in the waiting area during the actual examination.

Examination Results

Please note that results will neither be mailed nor provided by telephone.

Candidates and teachers can access examination marks online within approximately four weeks of the examination date. Access to complete examination results, with comments and marks, will be available no later than eight weeks after the examination date.

Teachers may access their students' examination results by visiting www.examinations.rcmusic.ca.

Official transcripts are available upon written request to The Royal Conservatory Examinations and payment of the requisite fee. (The Official Transcript Request Form may be downloaded from the website.)

Interpreting Examination Results

All candidates may access their complete, official results (including examiners' comments) online no later than eight weeks after the examination has taken place. The examiner's report explains how the final mark was calculated, and provides information to support candidates in their future musical development. The mark reflects the examiner's evaluation of the candidate's performance during the examination, which being a live performance, cannot be reconstructed. Appeals are considered only in the event of a serious procedural irregularity, and only upon completion of the official Appeals Process.

Classification of Marks

First Class Honors with Distinction	90–100
First Class Honors	80–89
Honors	70–79
Pass (Preparatory and Grades 1–10)	60

Marking Criteria for Performance of Repertoire

First Class Honors with Distinction: 90–100
This standing is awarded for exceptional performances that are confident and communicative, while demonstrating technical command, insightful awareness of style, and convincing musical interpretation.

First Class Honors: 80–89
This standing is awarded for performances that are musically engaging, show thoughtful preparation, and demonstrate technical security, stylistic understanding, and musical awareness. There is quick recovery from any minor slips or brief lapses.

Honors: 70–79
This standing is awarded for performances that are generally secure and fluent, indicate careful preparation, and reflect some awareness of style and musical understanding. There may be occasional slips or lapses, with room for further development of technical control and attention to musical details.

Pass: 60–69
This standing is awarded for performances that exhibit a basic level of preparation. There may be slips or lapses, loss of continuity, unresolved technical issues, and a lack of attention to musical details. The examiner's report will identify areas that require further study and exploration.

Fail: 50–59
The performance is a work in progress. There are many errors, slips, and stumbles disturbing the continuity. Although some aspects of the performance may show basic preparation, a satisfactory performance requires more consistent fluency and attention to both musical elements and markings in the score.

Marks Below 50
The performance is not yet ready for assessment due to insufficient preparation.

Login at rcmusic.ca to view online results

Table of Marks

	Prep–Grade 1	Grade 2	Grades 3–4	Grade 5	Grade 6	Grade 7	Grades 8–9	Grade 10	ARCT in Violin Performance
Repertoire	**60**	**60**	**60**	**60**	**60**	**50**	**50**	**50 (35)**	**80**
List A	27	27	18	17	17	15 (1.5)	15 (1.5)	15 (1.5)	20 (2)
List B	27	27	18	20	20	20	15	15	20
List C		–	18	17	17	15 (1.5)	10 (1)	10 (1)	20 (2)
List D		–	–	–	–	–	10 (1)	10 (1)	20 (2)
Memory	6 (3+3)	6 (3+3)	6 (2+2+2)	6 (3+3)	6 (3+3)	–	–	–	–
Orchestral Excerpts	–	–	–	–	–	**10**	**10**	**10 (7)**	**20**
Technical Requirements	**30**	**30**	**20**	**20**	**20**	**20**	**20**	**20 (14)**	–
Etudes	15	15	10	10	10	8	8	8	–
Technical Tests	15	15	10	10	10	12	12	12	–
Ear Tests	**10**	**10**	**10**	**10**	**10**	**10**	**10**	**10 (7)**	
Clapback	5	3	3	3	2	2	–	–	–
Intervals	–	3	3	3	3	3	3	2	–
Chords	–	–	–	–	2	2	2	2	–
Cadences	–	–	–	–	–	–	2	3	–
Playback	5	4	4	4	3	3	3	3	–
Sight Reading	–	–	**10**	**10**	**10**	**10**	**10**	**10 (7)**	–
Playing	–	–	7	7	7	7	7	7	–
Clapping	–	–	3	3	3	3	3	3	–
TOTALS	**100**	**100**	**100**	**100**	**100**	**100**	**100**	**100**	**100**

- The figures in parentheses for Lists A, C, and D indicate the marks that will be deducted for selections that are not memorized.
- Figures in bold parentheses indicate the minimum number of marks required to receive 70 percent.
- To qualify for the ARCT examination, Grade 10 candidates must achieve either an overall mark of 75 *or* a minimum of 70 percent in *each* section of the examination. (In the "Table of Marks," 70-percent figures are given in parentheses.)
- Candidates for the ARCT in Violin Performance must achieve an overall mark of 70 in order to pass.

Supplemental Examinations

Improve an Examination Mark

Candidates seeking to improve their overall mark at the Grade 10 level may take one or more Supplemental Examinations.

- Supplemental Examinations must be taken within two years of the original examination.
- Supplemental Examinations are given during regular examination sessions.
- Candidates in Grade 10 may repeat any *two* sections of a practical examination: Repertoire, Orchestral Excerpts, Technical Requirements, Ear Tests, or Sight Reading.
- To be eligible for a Supplemental Examination in Grade 10, candidates must achieve a minimum mark of 65 overall.

Candidates in Grade 10 must complete the Grade 10 theory co-requisites within five years of the *original practical examination,* not any subsequent supplemental examinations.

Split Grade 10 Practical Examinations

Beginning in the 2013–2014 academic year, candidates may choose to take the Grade 10 Violin examination in two separate segments: one consisting entirely of Repertoire; the other consisting of Technical Requirements, including Etudes and Technical Tests, as well as Ear Tests, Sight Reading, and Orchestral Excerpts. The division of material in the split Grade 10 examination cannot be altered. However, candidates may choose which segment to take first.

Candidates for the split Grade 10 examination must complete all practical examination requirements within two years of the initial examination segment. Candidates for the split Grade 10 examination may schedule their examinations within the same session or in different sessions; however, both segments of the split Grade 10 examination and any supplemental examinations must be completed within the two-year period. Candidates who choose the split format must complete both segments before registering for any supplemental examinations. All theoretical co-requisites for the Grade 10 examination must be completed within five years of the initial Grade 10 practical examination segment. Only candidates who take the complete Grade 10 examination (without the split) will be eligible to receive a Regional Gold Medal.

Practical Examination Certificates

Certificates are awarded to candidates who successfully complete the requirements for their Grade.

Beginning in Grade 5, certificates are awarded *after* the theory co-requisites for that Grade have been successfully completed. Theory co-requisites must be completed within five years of the original practical examination.

Please note that ARCT diplomas are awarded to candidates at the annual Convocation ceremony. Candidates may not use the official designation "ARCT" before Convocation.

Medals

The academic year runs from September to August. Each academic year, gold medals are awarded to the candidates who achieve exceptional examination results. No application is required.

Gold Medals

Gold medals are awarded by province or region to candidates in Preparatory and Grades 1 to 10 who receive the highest marks for their respective practical examination. To be eligible, a candidate must receive a minimum mark of 80 percent in the practical examination, and have completed all theory co-requisites for the respective Grade.

ARCT Gold Medals

A gold medal is awarded to the graduating ARCT in Violin Performance candidate who receives the highest mark across Canada for the practical examination. To be eligible, a candidate must receive:

- A minimum of 85 percent in the practical examination
- A minimum of 70 percent in each theory co-requisite examination

A gold medal for excellence in theory is also awarded to the graduating ARCT candidate who completes the theory examinations listed below with the highest average mark. To be eligible, a candidate must receive a minimum overall average of 80 percent for the eight examinations.

Basic Harmony *or* Basic Keyboard Harmony
Intermediate Harmony *or* Intermediate Keyboard Harmony
Advanced Harmony *or* Advanced Keyboard Harmony
Counterpoint
Analysis
History 1: An Overview
History 2: Middle Ages to Classical
History 3: 19th Century to Present

School Credits

The Royal Conservatory Examinations results can sometimes be used as a credit toward high school graduation or toward university entrance. In Canada, the policies of provincial education ministries can be found online under "Candidate Recognition, Accreditation." Candidates are advised to discuss the eligibility of their examination results with their school principal or guidance counsellor.

Musicianship Examinations

A musicianship examination may replace the Ear Tests section of a Grade 8, 9, 10, or ARCT in Violin Pedagogy examination. Please consult the current *Musicianship Syllabus* at www.examinations.rcmusic.ca for examination requirements. The musicianship examination must be taken at least one session *before* the practical examination.

Musicianship Grade	Practical Examination Grade
Junior Musicianship	Grade 8
Intermediate Musicianship	Grade 9
Senior Musicianship	Grade 10 and Teacher's ARCT

Candidates who have completed a musicianship examination should submit the following documentation when registering for the corresponding practical examination:

- a photocopy of the musicianship examination results
- a letter requesting exemption from the Ear Tests section of the upcoming practical examination

RESPs

Use of Education Funds for Music Studies

Candidates who have a Registered Education Savings Plan (RESP) may be eligible to use these funds to support private studies in music at the Grade 9, Grade 10, and/or ARCT levels. Candidates should consult their RESP providers for more information.

Editions

For many repertoire items, the *Syllabus* listing includes a suggested edition (indicated by an assigned publisher abbreviation). These editions have been chosen for their quality and for their availability in North America.

The Royal Conservatory strongly encourages the use of modern editions. These editions benefit from current scholarship and provide a reliable basis for study and performance. However, if a student has purchased an online edition or downloaded a free edition which is in the public domain, they must provide either proof of payment, in the case of purchased editions, or proof of legal, free download, in the case of online editions in the public domain.

Fingering, bowing, and other editorial markings vary from edition to edition. Examination marks will not be deducted for altering these editorial suggestions as long as the resulting change is musically acceptable.

Availability

The Royal Conservatory Examinations has made every effort to ensure that the materials listed in the *Violin Syllabus, 2013 Edition* are in print and available at leading music retailers throughout North America. If you experience difficulty in obtaining violin music in your community, you may visit www.frederickharrismusic.com to find a listing of additional music retailers near you.

Anthologies and Collections

If a repertoire selection is published in a collection of a composer's music or in an anthology containing music by a number of composers, the title of the collection or anthology is usually included in the *Syllabus* listing. Individual selections may also be found in other sources. In order to save space, the words "volume" and "book" have usually been omitted; a number following a title indicates the number of the volume, book, or set number in which a selection can be found (for example, *Suzuki Violin School, Revised Edition,* 2).

The Violin Series, 2013 Edition

In order to ensure the ready availability of high-quality examination materials, The Frederick Harris Music Co., Limited has published the *Violin Series, 2013 Edition*. This series includes nine volumes of *Violin Repertoire* (Preparatory through Grade 8) with compact discs; two volumes of *Violin Technique and Etudes* (Preparatory–4; Grades 5–8), and one volume of *Orchestral Excerpts* (Grades 7–ARCT).

Copyright and Photocopying

Federal and international copyright laws prohibit the use of photocopies without the permission of the publisher or website. The use of unauthorized photocopies for examination purposes constitutes copyright infringement as outlined in the Copyright Act of Canada. Additional information about federal copyright law is available online through the Copyright Board of Canada at www.cb-cda.gc.ca.

Candidates should bring all music to be performed to the examination. Candidates who wish to photocopy one page of a selection to facilitate a page turn must do so with permission from the publisher.

With this notice, The Frederick Harris Music Co., Limited grants permission to festival, recital, and examination participants to photocopy single pages from its publications to facilitate a page turn.

Please note that photocopied music will not be permitted in the examination room. Candidates who bring unauthorized photocopies to the examination will not be examined.

Abbreviations

Names of Publishers

The following abbreviations identify publishers listed throughout the *Violin Syllabus, 2013 Edition*. When no publisher or edition is indicated for a specific piece, the work is available in several standard editions. For more information, please see "Examination Repertoire" on p. 9.

ABR	Associated Board of the Royal Schools of Music
AEN	Aeneas Press
ALF	Alfred Publishing Co., Inc.
AUG	Augener & Co.
B&H	Boosey & Hawkes
B&V	Broekmans & Van Poppel
BAR	Bärenreiter
BEB	Bèrben Edizioni Musicali
BER	Berandol Music
BIL	G. Billaudot
BMC	Boston Music Company (Music Sales)
BOS	Bosworth (Music Sales)
BRH	Breitkopf & Härtel
BUT	Edition Butorac
CAN	Cantus Music
CHA	Chappell & Co., Inc. (Alfred)
CHD	Children's Music Series
CHS	Chester Music Ltd.
CMC	Canadian Music Centre Library
COM	Éditions Combre
DHM	DeHaske Music Publishing
DOM	Les Éditions Doberman-Yppan
DUR	Durand et Cie
ELK	Elkin Co. Music Publishers
EMA	European Music Archive (Spartan Press)
EMB	Editio Musica Budapest
EVO	Evocation Publishing
FAB	Faber Music Ltd.
FHM	The Frederick Harris Music Co., Limited
FIS	Carl Fischer Music
FRB	Francesco Bongiovanni
GIV	Givens Violinland
GVT	Gordon V. Thompson Music (Alfred)
HAL	Hal Leonard Corporation
HEN	G. Henle Verlag
IMS	IMSLP Petrucci Music Library
IND	École Vincent d'Indy
INT	International Music
KAL	Edwin F. Kalmus
KJO	Neil A. Kjos Music Company
KMA	Kevin Mayhew
LEE	Leeds Music (Canada)
LIM	Lime Green Music
MAS	Masters Music Publications
MPB	M.P. Belaieff
MUZ	Muzyka Moscow
NOV	Novello
OSS	Ossian
OTT	Schott Music GmbH
OUP	Oxford University Press
PER	Peer International
PET	Edition Peters
PRE	Theodore Presser Company
PWM	Polskie Wydawnictwo Muzyczne
RIC	G. Ricordi
S&B	Stainer & Bell
SCH	G. Schirmer Inc.
SIK	Sikorski
SIM	N. Simrock Publishers
UMP	United Music Publishers
UNI	Universal Edition Inc.
WAR	Warner Bros. Publications
WAT	Waterloo Music Co. (Mayfair)
WIL	Willis Music
ZAN	Zanibon
ZIM	Musikverlag Zimmerman Frankfurt

Other Abbreviations and Symbols

arr.	arranged by
attr.	attributed to
ed.	edited by
m., mm.	measure (s)
no.	number
op.	opus
p., pp.	page(s)
rev.	revised
trans.	translated by
transc.	transcribed by
vol.	volume

●	represents one selection for examination purposes
▶	selection is published in *Violin Series, 2013 Edition* FHM

Thematic Catalogues

Opus Numbers and Catalogue Numbers

"Opus" (op.) is a term used with a number to designate the position of a given work in the chronological sequence of works by the composer. However, these numbers are often an unreliable guide, and may have been assigned by a publisher rather than the composer. Sometimes a single work will have conflicting opus numbers. Works in certain genres, such as operas, were not always assigned opus numbers. For these reasons, individual works by a number of composers are identified by numbers assigned in scholarly thematic catalogues. A number of the more important thematic catalogues are listed below.

Johann Sebastian Bach

Works by J.S. Bach are identified by "BWV" numbers (for example, Partita No. 2 in D Minor, BWV 1004). "BWV" is the abbreviation for *Bach-Werke-Verzeichnis,* the short title of the *Thematisch-systematisches Verzeichnis der musikalischen Werke von Johann Sebastian Bach* (Leipzig, 1950), a thematic catalogue of Bach's complete works originally compiled by the German music librarian Wolfgang Schmieder.

George Frideric Handel

Works by George Frideric Handel are identified by "HWV" numbers (for example, Sonata No. 2 in G Minor, HWV 368). "HWV" is an abbreviation for *Handel Werke Verzeichnis.* The full title for this thematic catalogue, compiled by Margaret and Walter Eisen, is *Händel-Handbuch, gleichzeitig Suppl. zu Hallische Händel-Ausgabe* (Kassel: Bärenreiter, 1978–1986).

Franz Joseph Haydn

Works by Haydn are identified by Hoboken numbers (for example, String Quartet in C Major ("The Bird"), Hob. III:39). Anthony van Hoboken was a Dutch musicologist. His thematic catalogue, *Joseph Haydn: Thematisch-bibliographisches Werkverzeichnis* (Mainz, B. Schott, 1957–1971) divides Haydn's works into a number of categories that are indicated by Roman numerals.

Wolfgang Amadeus Mozart

Works by Mozart are identified by "K" numbers (for example, Symphony No. 25 in G Minor, K 183). "K" stands for Köchel Verzeichnis, first published in 1862. Ludwig Ritter von Köchel (1800–1877) was an Austrian professor of botany who devoted his retirement years to collecting all the known works by Mozart. He created a chronological catalogue in which these works are listed and numbered.

Franz Schubert

Works by Schubert are identified by "Deutsch" numbers (for example, String Quartet No. 14 in D Minor ("Death and the Maiden"), D 810). These numbers were assigned by Otto Erich Deutsch (1883–1967) in his thematic catalogue of Schubert's works, *Thematisches Verzeichnis seiner Werke in chronologischer Folge (Neue Schubert Ausgabe* Serie VIII, Bd. 4, Kassell, 1978).

Georg Philipp Telemann

Works by Telemann are identified by "TWV" numbers (for example, Sonata in F Major, TWV 41:F1). "TWV" is an abbreviation for *Telemann Werkverzeichnis.* This thematic catalogue—*Thematischer-Systematisches Verzeichnis seiner Werke: Telemann Werkverzeichnis* (Kassel: Barenreiter, 1984)—was compiled by Martin Runke.

Antonio Vivaldi

Works by Vivaldi are identified by "RV" numbers and/or by "F" numbers (for example, Concerto in A Minor, op. 3, no. 6, RV 356/F I:176). RV is an abbreviation for *Ryom Verzeichnis*. This thematic catalogue of Vivaldi's works—*Verzeichnis der Werke Antonio Vivaldis: kleine Ausgabe* (Leipzig: Deutscher Verlag für Musik, 1974, 2nd ed. 1979) was compiled by Peter Ryom. The F numbers were assigned by Antonio Fanna in *Opere strumentali di Antonio Vivaldi (1678–1741): catalogo numerico-tematico secondo la catalogazione Fanna* (Milan, 1986).

Anhang

Some catalogue numbers include the prefix "Anh." (for example, *Notenbuch der Anna Magdalena Bach*, BWV Anh. 114). "Anh." is an abbreviation for Anhang, a German word meaning appendix or supplement.

WoO

Some catalogue numbers include the prefix "WoO" (for example, *Sechs Menuette*, WoO 10 by Ludwig van Beethoven). "WoO" is an abbreviation for Werk ohne Opuszahl (work without opus number). These numbers are used to designate works for which the composer did not assign an opus number.

Resources

The following texts are useful for reference, teaching, and examination preparation. No single text is necessarily complete for examination purposes, but these recommended reading and resource lists are an indispensable source of:

- teaching tips for all ages and abilities
- tips for interpretation of repertoire
- tools for better sight reading
- advice on fostering talent in young people
- supplemental teaching material to support and enhance the *Violin Syllabus, 2013 Edition*

General Resources

Violin Series, 2013 Edition

Violin Series, 2013 Edition: Violin Repertoire. 9 vols. (Preparatory–Level 8) with compact discs. Toronto, ON: The Frederick Harris Music Co., Limited, 2013.

Violin Series, 2013 Edition: Violin Technique and Etudes. 2 vols. (Preparatory–4; 5–8). Toronto, ON: The Frederick Harris Music Co., Limited, 2013.

Violin Series, 2013 Edition: Orchestral Excerpts (Levels 7–ARCT). Toronto, ON: The Frederick Harris Music Co., Limited, 2013.

Sight Reading and Ear Training

Berlin, Boris, and Andrew Markow. *Ear Training for Practical Examinations: Melody Playback/Singback.* 4 vols. (Levels 1–ARCT). Toronto, ON: The Frederick Harris Music Co., Limited, 1986–1988.

———. *Ear Training for Practical Examinations: Rhythm Clapback/Singback.* 3 vols. (Levels 1–7). Toronto, ON: The Frederick Harris Music Co., Limited, 1989–1991.

Braaten, Brenda, and Crystal Wiksyk. *Sound Advice: Theory and Ear Training* (Levels 1–8) (Online audio tracks at www.soundadvicedirect.com). Toronto, ON: The Frederick Harris Music Co., Limited, 2005–2006.

Harris, Paul. *Improve your Sight-reading! A Workbook for Examinations.* London: Faber, 1994.

Hindemith, Paul. *Elementary Training for Musicians.* 2nd ed. London: Schott, 1974.

Kember, John, Roger Smith, and Marguerite Wilkinson. *Violin Sight-Reading.* 2 vols. Mainz, Schott, 2006–2007.

Martin, Joanne. *I Can Read Music: A Note-reading Book for Violin Students.* 2 vols. Van Nuys, CA: Alfred Publishing Co., Inc. First published Miami, FL: Summy-Birchard, 1991, 1997.

Nelson, Sheila. *Flip-A-Rhythm.* 2 vols. London: Boosey & Hawkes, 1995.

Schlosar, Carol. *Comprehensive Ear Training, Professional Series* 11 vols. (Levels 1–ARCT) (Book with CD). Toronto, ON: The Frederick Harris Music Co., Limited. First published Sicamous, BC: Keystroke Publishing, 1993.

———. *Comprehensive Ear Training: Student Series.* 11 compact discs (Levels 1–ARCT). Toronto, ON: The Frederick Harris Music Co., Limited. First published Sicamous, BC: Keystroke Publishing, 1998.

Official Examination Papers

The Royal Conservatory Examinations Official Examination Papers. 15 vols. Toronto, ON: The Frederick Harris Music Co., Limited, published annually.

- Basic Rudiments
- Intermediate Rudiments
- Advanced Rudiments
- Introductory Harmony
- Basic Harmony
- Basic Keyboard Harmony
- History 1: An Overview
- Intermediate Harmony
- Intermediate Keyboard Harmony
- History 2: Middle Ages to Classical
- Counterpoint
- Advanced Harmony
- Advanced Keyboard Harmony
- History 3: 19th Century to Present
- Analysis

General Reference Works

Burkholder, J. Peter, Donald J. Grout, and Claude V. Palisca. *A History of Western Music.* 8th ed. New York: Norton, 2009.

Freymuth, Malva. *Mental Practice and Imagery for Musicians.* Boulder, CO: Integrated Musician's Press, 1999.

Green, Barry and W. Timothy Gallwey. *The Inner Game of Music.* New York: Doubleday, 1986.

Horvath, Janet. *Playing (Less) Hurt: An Injury Prevention Guide for Musicians.* Milwaukee, WI: Hal Leonard, 2010.

Kallmann, Helmut, Gilles Potvin, and Kenneth Winters, eds. *Encyclopedia of Music in Canada.* 2nd ed. Toronto, ON: University of Toronto Press, 1992. (Available online at www.thecanadianencyclopedia.com.)

Kamien, Roger. *Music: An Appreciation.* 9th ed. New York: McGraw-Hill, 2008.

Latham, Alison, ed. *The Oxford Companion to Music.* Oxford: Oxford University Press, 2002.

Machlis, Joseph, and Kristine Forney. *The Enjoyment of Music.* 11th ed. New York: Norton, 2011.

Paull, Barbara, and Christine Harrison. *The Athletic Musician: A Guide to Playing Without Pain.* Lanham, MD: Scarecrow Press, 1997.

Randel, Don Michael, ed. *The Harvard Biographical Dictionary of Music.* Cambridge, MA: Harvard University Press, 1996.

———. *The Harvard Dictionary of Music.* 4th ed. Cambridge, MA: Belknap Press of Harvard University Press, 2003.

Sadie, Stanley, ed. *The New Grove Dictionary of Musical Instruments.* 3 vols. London: Macmillan, 1993.

Sadie, Stanley, and John Tyrell, eds. *The New Grove Dictionary of Music and Musicians.* 2nd ed., 29 vols. London: Macmillan, 2001. (Also available online.)

Slonimsky, Nicolas, ed. emeritus. *Baker's Biographical Dictionary of Music and Musicians.* Centennial ed. 6 vols. New York: Schirmer, 2001.

Stolba, K. Marie. *The Development of Western Music: A History.* 3rd ed. Boston, MA: McGraw-Hill, 1998.

Violin Resources

Etudes and Technique

Barber, Barbara. *Scales for Advanced Violinists.* Van Nuys, CA: Alfred Publishing Co., Inc., 2005.

Bauer, John. *Progressive Scale Studies for Violin.* Pacific, MO: Mel Bay, 1998.

Bériot, Charles-Auguste de. *The First Thirty Concert Studies for the Violin,* op. 123. New York: G. Schirmer, 1939, 1967.

Cohen, Mary. *Scaley Monsters.* London: Faber Music, 1994.

Dancla, Charles. *Thirty-six Melodious and Easy Studies,* op. 84. Mainz: Schott, 2011.

———. *20 Études brillantes et caractéristiques,* op. 73. Budapest: Editio Musica Budapest, 1980.

de Keyser, Paul. *Violin Study Time.* London: Faber Music, 1988.

Dont, Jacob. *Thirty Progressive Excercises for the Violin (With Accompaniment of a Second Violin),* op. 38. New York: G. Schirmer, 1967.

Dounis, Demetrius. *The Dounis Collection: Eleven Books of Studies for the Violin.* New York: Carl Fischer, 2005.

Flesch, Carl. *Scale System.* New York: Carl Fischer, 1926.

Galamian, Ivan. *Contemporary Violin Technique.* 2 vols. New York: Galaxy Music Corp., 1966.

Gaviniès, Pierre. *24 études (matinées).* Peters; New York: International Music, 1963.

Harris, Paul. *Improve Your Scales!* 4 vols. London: Faber Music, 1996.

Hrimaly, Jan. *Scale Studies for Violin.* New York: G. Schirmer, 1986.

Locatelli, Pietro. *The Art of the Violin: 24 Caprices for Solo Violin,* op. 3. Milan: Ricordi, 1920.

Minsky, Aaron. *Ten American Violin Etudes.* Oxford: Oxford University Press, 2011.

O'Reilly, Sally. *Fiddle Magic: 180 Technical Exercises for Violin.* San Diego, CA: Neil A. Kjos Music Company, 1991.

———. *String Rhythms.* San Diego, CA: Neil A. Kjos Music Company, 1992.

Sassmannshaus, Kurt. *Early Start on the Violin.* 4 vols. Kassel: Bärenreiter: 2008.

Schradieck, Henry. *School of Violin Technique.* 4 vols. New York: G. Schirmer, 1928.

Ševčík Otakar. *Analytical Studies and Exercises,* opp. 16–21. 6 vols. Lauren Keiser Music Publishing, 2012.

———. *School of Bowing Technique,* op. 2. 6 vols. London: Bosworth, 1901.

———. *School of Violin Technique,* op. 1. 4 vols. London: Bosworth, 1901.

———. *Violin Studies: Changes of Position and Preparatory Scale Exercises,* op. 8. London: Bosworth, 1901.

———. *Violin Studies: Preparatory Studies in Double-Stopping,* op. 9. London: Bosworth, 1901.

———. *Violin Studies: Preparatory Trill Studies,* op. 7. 2 vols. London: Bosworth, 1901.

Skelton, Robert. *The Complete Violin Technique Book.* Toronto, ON: The Frederick Harris Music Co., Limited, 1998.

Suzuki, Shinichi. *Position Etudes, Revised Edition.* Van Nuys, CA: Alfred Publishing Co., Inc. First published Miami, FL: Summy-Birchard, 1973.

———. *Tonalization.* Van Nuys, CA: Alfred Publishing Co., Inc. First published Miami, FL: Summy-Birchard, 1955.

Tartini, Giuseppe. *The Art of Bowing for the Violin.* Facsimile reprint. New York: G. Schirmer, 1909, 1967.

Wieniawski, Henryk. *Etudes-Caprices,* op. 10. New York: International Music, 1973.

———. *Etudes-Caprices,* op. 18. New York: International Music, 1974.

Whistler, Harvey S. *Introducing the Positions.* 2 vols. Chicago, IL: Rubank Publications, 1944–46.

Orchestral Excerpts

Adey, Christopher. *Orchestral Performance*. London: Faber and Faber, 1998.
Bach, Johann Sebastian. *Violin Solos from the Sacred Cantatas, Masses, Passions and Oratorios*. Ed. Martin Wolfhurst. Kassel: Bärenreiter, 1996.
Boerries, Karin. *Test Pieces for Orchestral Auditions*. 2 vols. Mainz: Schott, 1994.
Gingold, Josef, ed. *Orchestral Excerpts from the Symphonic Repertoire*. 3 vols. New York: International, 1953–1962.
Green, Elizabeth A.H. *Orchestral Bowings and Routines*. American String Teachers Association, 1957. Distributed by Alfred Publishing Co., Inc., 2010.
Strauss, Richard. *Orchestral Excerpts from Symphonic Works: For Violin*. Ed. Prill. New York: International, 1944.
Wulfhurst, Martin. *The Orchestral Violinist's Companion*. 2 vols. Barenreiter, 2012.
The Orchestral Musician's CD-ROM Library. 10 vols. CD Sheet Music, 2007.

Violin Reference Works

Arditti, Irvine and Robert Platz. *The Techniques of Violin Playing*. Kassel: Barenreiter, 2012.
Auer, Leopold. *Violin Master Works and Their Interpretation*. London: Dover, 2012.
———. *Violin Playing As I Teach It*. London: Gerald Duckworth, 1921, 1960, 1980.
Bachmann, Alberto A. *An Encyclopedia of the Violin*. New York: D. Appleton, 1929, 1937, 1975; London: Dover, 2008.
Baillot, Pierre. *The Art of the Violin*. Trans. Louise Goldberg. Evanston, IL: Northwestern University Press, 1991.
Barber, Barbara. *Fingerboard Geography for Violin*. Van Nuys, CA: Alfred Publishing Co., Inc., 2008.
Barrett, Carolyn M. *The Magic of Matsumoto: The Suzuki Method of Education*. Palm Springs, CA: ETC Publications, 1995.
Berman, Joel, Barbara Jackson, and Kenneth Sarch. *Dictionary of Bowing and Pizzicato Terms*. 4th ed. American String Teachers Association, 1957. Distributed by Alfred Publishing Co., Inc., 2010.
Boyden, David Dodge. *History of Violin Playing from its Origins to 1761*. London: Oxford University Press, 1965, 1975; Oxford: Clarendon Press, 1990.
———, et al. *The New Grove Violin Family*. New York, W.W. Norton and Co., 1989.
Cook, Clifford A. *Suzuki Education in Action*. New York: Exposition Press, 1970.
Courvoisier, Karl. *The Technique of Violin Playing: The Joachim Method*. London: Dover, 2006.
Donington, Robert. *String Playing in Baroque Music*. London: Faber and Faber, 1977.
Fischer, Simon. *Basics: 300 Exercises & Practice Routines for the Violin*. London: Peters Edition Limited, 1997.
———. *Practice: 250 Step-by-step Practice Methods for the Violin*. London: Peters Edition Limited, 2004.
———. *Scales: Scales and Scale Studies for the Violin*. London: Peters Edition Limited, 2012.
Flesch, Carl. *The Art of Violin Playing*. 2 vols. Trans. and ed. Eric Rosenblith. New York: Carl Fischer, 2000.
Galamian, Ivan. *Principles of Violin Playing and Teaching*. 3rd ed. Ann Arbor, MI: Shar Products, 1999; London: Dover, 2013.
Gerle, Robert. *The Art of Practising the Violin*. London: Stainer & Bell, Ltd., 1983, 1985.
Goldberg, Milton. *The Violin Column*. Boulder, CO: Suzuki Association of the Americas, 1984.
Havas, Kató. *A New Approach to Violin Playing*. London: Bosworth, 1961, 1970.
———. *The Twelve Lesson Course in a New Approach to Violin Playing*. London: Bosworth, 1964.
Hermann, Evelyn. *Shinichi Suzuki: The Man and His Life*. Rev. ed. Miami, FL: Summy-Birchard, 1995.
Kendall, John. *The Suzuki Violin Method in American Music Education*. Rev. ed. Miami, FL: Summy-Birchard, 1985.
Kolneder, Walter. *The Amadeus Book of the Violin: Construction, History, and Music*. Trans. and ed. Reinhard G. Pauly. Portland, OR: Amadeus Press, 1972, 1998, 2003.

Kreitman, Edward. *Teaching From the Balance Point: A Guide for Suzuki Parents, Teachers, and Students.* Western Springs, IL: Western Springs School of Talent Education, 1998.

Loft, Abram. *Violin and Keyboard: the Duo Repertoire: from the 17th Century to Mozart.* 2 vols. Portland, OR: Amadeus Press, 2003.

Martens, Frederick H. *Violin Mastery: Interviews with Heifetz, Auer, Kriesler and Others.* London: Dover, 2006.

Menuhin, Yehudi. *Violin: Six Lessons with Yehudi Menuhin.* London: Faber Music, 1971, 1981.

Mozart, Leopold. *Treatise of the Fundamental Principles of Violin Playing.* Trans. Editha Knocker. 2nd ed. Oxford: Oxford University Press, 1951, 1985.

Pernecky, Jack M. *Teaching the Fundamentals of Violin Playing.* Ed. Lorraine Fink. Van Nuys, CA: Alfred Publishing Co., Inc. First published Miami, FL: Summy-Birchard, 1998.

Rapoport, Katharine. *Violin for Dummies.* 2nd ed. Toronto, ON: Wiley, 2012.

Rolland, Paul. *Basic Principles of Violin Playing.* American String Teachers Association, 1959. Distributed by Alfred Publishing Co., Inc., 2010.

———. *The Teaching of Action in String Playing.* Urbana, IL: Illinois String Research Associates, 1974, 2000.

Rosenblith, Eric. *Ah, You Play the Violin…: Thoughts along the Path to Musical Artistry.* New York: Carl Fischer, 2010.

Starr, William, ed. *The Suzuki Violinist.* Knoxville, TN: Kingston Ellis Press, 1976.

Stowell, Robin. *The Cambridge Companion to the Violin.* Cambridge: Cambridge University Press, 1992.

Suzuki, Shinichi. *Ability Development From Age Zero.* Miami, FL: Summy-Birchard, 1981.

———. *Man and Talent: Search into the Unknown.* Ann Arbor, MI: Shar Products, 1990.

———. *Nurtured By Love: A New Approach to Education.* Miami, FL: Summy-Birchard, 1983.

———. *Where Love Is Deep: The Writings of Shinichi Suzuki.* St. Louis, MO: Talent Education Journal Press, 1982.

———. *Young Children's Talent Education and Its Method.* Trans. Kyoko Selden. Miami, FL: Summy-Birchard, 1996.

Szende, Ottó and Mihály Nemessuri. *The Physiology of Violin Playing.* London: Collet's, 1971.

Szigeti, Joseph. *Szigeti on the Violin.* London: Dover, 1969, 1979.

———. *A Violinist's Notebook.* London: Gerald Duckworth, 1964.

Timmerman, Craig. *Journey Down the Kreisler Highway: Reflections on the Teachings of Shinichi Suzuki.* Memphis, TN: Ivory Palaces Music, 1987.

Yampolsky, I.M. *The Principles of Violin Fingering.* London: Oxford University Press, 1967, 1984.

Web Resources

Alliance for Canadian New Music Projects (ACNMP): www.acnmp.ca
American String Teachers Association (ASTA): www.astaweb.com
Canadian Federation of Music Teachers' Associations (CFMTA): www.cfmta.org
Canadian Music Centre (CMC): www.musiccentre.ca
Mimi Zweig String Pedagogy: www.stringpedagogy.com
Music Teachers National Association (MTNA): www.mtna.org
National Association for Music Education (NAfME): www.nafme.org
The Sassmannshaus Tradition for Violin Playing: www.violinmasterclass.com
Suzuki Association of the Americas: www.suzukiassociation.org
The Violin Community: www.violinist.com
Violin Excerpts: www.violinexcerpts.com
The Violin Lab: www.violinlab.com
Violin Online: www.violinonline.com
Violinist in Balance: www.violinistinbalance.nl

Frequently Asked Questions

Practical Examinations

What is a practical examination?

A practical examination is an assessment of repertoire, etudes, technique, ear training, and sight reading for a musical instrument, voice, or speech arts and drama.

How can I obtain permission to photocopy an out-of-print selection that I find in a library or receive from a teacher?

Contact the publisher to request permission to make an authorized photocopy. Contact information for most publishers can be found online or obtained from a music retailer. Some music retailers can obtain authorized photocopies through a special online service.

Can I photocopy a page of music to facilitate a page turn?

You may photocopy a single page once you have obtained permission from the publisher. With this notice, The Frederick Harris Music Co., Limited grants permission to festival, recital, and examination participants to photocopy single pages from their publications to facilitate a page turn.

How do I choose the best edition for a piece?

The best editions often have minimal editorial markings. These editions, often called Urtext, are available from most music retailers. If you are unsure about the best edition, ask your music retailer for suggestions.

Should candidates follow repeat signs? *Da capo* markings?

Candidates should observe *da capo* markings at an examination performance. Repeat signs should usually be ignored; however, repeat signs should be observed if indicated in a footnote below the music in the *Violin Series, 2013 Edition* or if indicated in the *Violin Syllabus, 2013 Edition.*

Why are teachers and parents not allowed in the room during practical examinations?

Practical examinations provide a unique opportunity for candidates to perform in a highly focused, one-on-one environment, without distraction.

Where can I find recordings of examination repertoire?

Violin Series, 2013 Edition includes compact discs containing piano accompaniments for *Violin Repertoire* from Preparatory to Grade 8. A compact disc is included with the purchase of each *Violin Repertoire* book.

What do I do if I have an emergency situation on the day of my examination and I need to cancel?

Contact the Examination Centre Representative listed on your Examination Schedule by phone *as soon as possible*.

Theory Co-requisites

What is a theory co-requisite?

A theory co-requisite is a theory examination that must be completed before or within five years of the practical examination if the candidate wishes to receive a certificate for the practical examination. Candidates are encouraged to begin theory studies as early as possible.

Do I have to take theory examinations if I don't need a violin examination certificate?

You may take a violin examination at any grade except ARCT without fulfilling theory requirements. If you later decide that you would like to receive a certificate, you have five years from the date of the violin examination to fulfill the theory requirements. Candidates must complete prerequisite examinations in theory at least one session prior to attempting the ARCT in Violin Performance or the Teacher's ARCT.

Where can I find sample theory examination papers?

Official Examination Papers are published annually by The Frederick Harris Music Co., Limited to aid with examination preparation. Each book includes three examinations from the previous December, May, and August examination sessions plus an additional examination created for extra practice. Editions for three academic years are available at any given time and may be purchased from your local music retailer.

Practical Examination Day Checklist for Candidates

Before You Leave Home

___ Plan to arrive 15 minutes early.

___ Complete your Examination Program Form.

___ Bring original copies of all the music being performed in the examination.

___ Mark the pieces being performed with a paper clip or a "sticky note."

___ Bring an additional copy of any repertoire you are not performing from memory.

Points to Remember

- Photo ID may be requested before a candidate is admitted to the examination room.
- Photocopied music is prohibited unless authorized by the publisher.
- Recording devices are strictly prohibited in the examination room.
- Electronic devices, books, notes, bags, and coats must be left in the area designated by the Centre Representative.
- Parents, other family members, friends, and teachers must wait in the designated waiting area.
- Standing and listening outside the examination room door is prohibited.
- The performance of repertoire may be interrupted by the examiner when an assessment has been made.

What to Expect from a Violin Examination

- A friendly, professional atmosphere.
- The undivided attention of an examiner.
- An objective assessment of your performance of repertoire, etudes, technique, ear tests, and sight reading.
- The examiner's written evaluation online within eight weeks of the examination.

After the Examination

Access your examination marks and examiner comments through the "Examination Results" link on the Royal Conservatory Examinations website (www.examinations.rcmusic.ca) approximately eight weeks after the examination.